A Matter of Time

A MATTER OF TIME

How Time Preferences Make or Break Civilization

ORWELL & GOODE

CONTENTS

INTRODUCTION

"Imagine there's no heaven"
—John Lennon

OTHER THAN ONE'S LIFE, the most important thing one can give is time—as time is a portion of one's life. In John Lennon's charttopper, "Imagine", seemingly lies the Western world's philosophy in approaching time—in living for today. And, as a foundation to this "living for today" philosophy, there necessarily needs to be a lack of consequences for one's actions; or an illusion of an absence of consequences. The living for today credo is misinterpresented as if tomorrow doesn't come. And while it's *true* that tomorrow hasn't revealed itself to us—yet—as it doesn't exist—yet—remember: tomorrow eventually comes. Tomorrow always comes. Tomorrow is unforgiving. Tomorrow is pissed because you didn't respect today. Tomorrow is when the piper will be paid. Tomorrow is when all those cheques written by your actions will bounce. And there will be consequences. You, yourself, may not feel the brunt of those consequences, but your children and children's children will.

To deny tomorrow is to deny reality. We'll just have to see what curveballs are thrown at us when tomorrow comes. Accepting reality for what it is can be hard when prevailing social norms dictate a narrative—for political ends—which orbit outside of the realm of reality and live under the guise or disguise of progress. But to deny consequences is to deny reality. It is to act on impulse; to throw caution into the wind. Urinating upwind will have messy consequences. But we've been told that the alarmists who raise awareness of those consequences are at fault. They're uncool, bigoted, prudish, boring, lame, unhip, squares. Many are floating, at their peril, in outer space. Those calling them back to earth are the ones in the wrong. Like a parent who rushes to stop their child inserting their fingers in a mains, those hinting at the waywardness of others are balked at. Now, the toddler is armed with an advanced vocabulary and can guilt the parent when the parent attempts to intervene. The parent, may not be able to vocalize their concern for the toddler's wellbeing, but has the toddler's wellbeing at heart. The parent has to stand back and watch the toddler electrocute himself and is called all sorts of names while picking up the toddler's medical bill.

In this day and age, consequences are externalized. You can stick your finger in the socket and somebody else will pick up the tab. And heck, why stop at your finger? There are other appendages you can insert in the socket! It's all good, bro, society has got you covered. And if they don't, enough political activism will ensure that a social program to protect you from the consequences of your actions will appear sooner rather than later.

There most certainly festers a pervasive illusion of a lack of consequences for one's actions: a bloated and sclerotic welfare state; social security and state pensions; the philosophical death of God; the pill; abortion clinics; to name a few. The prevailing view is that all of the aforementioned things are good, positive, and irreplaceable. I would like to suggest—perhaps controversially—that the above are contradictory to a functioning, healthy, and cohesive society. The "State", almost inevitably, replaced God with the decline of Christendom and the emergence of the industrialized modern world. But, with this transition from a transcendental being to haughty career bureaucrats, the "State" has pilfered God's omnipotence. The "State" has now become the invaluable mediator and panacea of all social issues or ills. As a way to balance this socially precarious tightrope act, the younger generations in particular, must be kept in a permanent state of childhood. In a quasi-Platonic manner, the State raises the kids, but not for their improvement or transformation into upstanding citizens or fearless warriors; but to create armies of cowardly, quivering, childlike consumerist taxstock. The State is now daddy. But to say "daddy" is patriarchal and, therefore, problematic. The State has assumed the role of the father in numerous family. The State is the provider and the protector. It projects an illusion of security and socialization of consequence. The State is an aegis to the modern broken family structure. The nuclear family is an existential competitor to modern Nanny State. Even as a provider, the modern State is inadequate. Like a pusher, it keeps its subjects dependent on hand outs. It requires a constant expansion of its tax stock via immigration.

Western welfare states are technically insolvent, but they have to bend the rules to continually deny reality like a tarp protecting a house of cards on a windy day. At what point will reality come to collect its dues? Many would be incapable to live their lives unassisted. Power-hungry politicians who promised largesse in exchange for status are long gone. To tell the addict to go cold turkey or else, won't be met with praise, but scorn; even though the addict, in the back of his mind, knows that his addiction will end him. No politician drawing attention to the economic denial of reality—national debts, debt-to-gdp ratio, welfare consumer to producer ratio, etc—would, in a million years, get elected. What happens when the chickens come home to roost?

But it isn't just the State which requires the populace to live for today. Modern multinational corporations bankroll self-serving politicians into office, who in turn enact favorable policies towards profit maximization. Most establishment-approved politicians are in the pockets of megacorporations and other interest groups who strive to cement a certain style of monopoly pertinent to their field of expertise. Megacorporations require fiscal and monetary policies to prompt increased sales, and immigration and social policies to lower wages while boosting productivity. All in all, the consumer, or more precisely, 'consuming-producer' is the one who loses; while being told by the media, entertainment, and the intelligentsia that their lifestyles and the government's policies partially supporting their lifestyles are, in fact, wonderful. But don't rock the boat. You'll be dealt with vitriol and bile. You'll uncover the wrath of social activists who'll aim to silence you by whichever means necessary. And ironically, many of the social activists who will paint you out as irreconcilably evil, despite their utopian views supposedly opposed the Establishment's interests, will find themselves being the extrajudicial enforcers for the Establishment.

The unholy matrimony of modern megacorporation and postnational (globalist) Western state has spelled the rapid decline of Western society. The State, in a sense, has become God and the products sold by megacorporation serve little more than temporary fixes for the spiritual void since the philosophical death of God. From such a massive detranscendentalization of values, time preferences have risen, given the fact that life expectancies have spiritually shortened and a greater meaning has been ripped away. Within that loss of meaning, living for tomorrow becomes less appealing. Meaning now comes from without: through material goods and experiences. Value is assigned through pricing instead of something more sentimental or immaterial.

Consequences are good, actually. Without conse-quences, maturity and wisdom would be impossible. Consequences aren't to be feared. Only those who recognize guilt for their actions stave off consequences. Reality has to be reified to fit a lifestyle where actions—for one recognizes a lingering guilt—are not only free from consequences; but also trendy, desirable, and socially ahead of the curve. Those aware of the finite nature of their own physical time attempt to excuse actions which may carry unwanted consequences; and invert preexisting value systems in order to do so. To attempt to minimize the consequences for the actions they'd rather externalize onto society or rationalize through abstraction are the pinnacle of selfishness while unintentionally minimizing their own humanity.

My goal in this book is to attempt to demonstrate the problems with high social time preferences. Civilization and high time preferences simply don't mix. Civilization cannot survive if everyone lives for today. What will there be for tomorrow? Civilization, in a way, is a living organism. What will happen if immediate pleasure overtakes the importance of its preservation? Like vultures, many have taken to feasting on the twitching corpse of Western Civilization—killed by two avoidable wars, self-serving politicians, utopian social engineering, and the introduction of socially carcinogenic forms of entertainment to pass the time in many meaningless lives when one isn't working to beef up profit margins or GDP. The character of those who inherited civilization, while never experiencing true hardship, take the civilization they've inherited for granted. They are not, sadly, cut from the same cloth as their ancestors who toiled laboriously in order to provide a stable and rich society. One striking difference is the amazing wealth that today's individual enjoys which frees him from the need to defer gratification, when everything can be had today; while a few generations ago, the deferral of gratification was necessary due to the cost and lack of availability of certain goods imposing rigid incentive structures which limited consumerism to a certain degree.

I also aim to explore what things—consumer goods, technology, social norms, etc—at people's disposal may turn them away from looking towards the future in favor of consumption or enjoyment today. It would seem that, naturally, in a more primitive state, people would prefer to consume now rather than in the future. The deferral of gratification (as I shall call it henceforth), requires discipline, intelligence, and perhaps some present suffering; however, in the long run, may prove beneficial to the person who shuns present consumption for future gratification. This, of course, can range from a variety of actions from storing food for the winter in a harsh climate to making a long term investment. Sure, in the first instance it's a matter of life and death, but in the second, it means to be materially wealthier in the future when the amount invested could've been used for, say, a night out and a deposit on a car. But, herein lies the issue: it appears as if more and more would rather take a night out and a deposit on a car than to squirrel their resources away for a rainy day or for their children's education, for example. And, lamentably, it doesn't end with financial decision making either, as individuals seemingly invest less and less time in forming relationships with their neighbors. As a result, social cohesion declines, solidarity wanes, and distrust metastasizes. One can only imagine what happens next.

Now, many people lead unfulfilling and inauthentic lives, but can get anything they desire—provided they have the funds—at the touch of a button, with delivery services falling over themselves to deliver the desired product with minimal waiting times. Modern life, for many, can be distilled into an oscillation between production and palliative consumption, punctuated with corporate 'package holiday' vacations to get away from it all—a life of production. Working a deadend corporate job 40 hours a week for a massive, faceless, indifferent, multinational; followed by watching vapid TV shows and chores for a couple of hours an evening, and salivating over a marginally updated overpriced gadget every so often isn't much of existence. What's the point of getting up in the morning to get that bread if there isn't much to do? Modern life is on course to become a series of external stimuli as a means to temporarily dispel boredom until we die. Life isn't being lived. Thanks to the marvellous growth of technology, life is being lived for us. Ironically, we are returning to a more primitive state as social norms and technology at our disposal, renders certain human qualities obsolete. And although life is becoming easier, people as individuals, are losing many of their faculties to technology. For westerners, in particular, the incentive structures or choices provided to them are presentminded. Impulse control is becoming something of a relic as gratification has become more instant. The wealth and technology we now enjoy has surpassed the wildest dreams of old utopian thinkers. But no matter how good we have it materially, sadness and social alienation are on the rise while the life expectancy of certain Western demographics appear to have peaked. If this is the best its ever been then why do so many feel blue? We were led to believe a booming GDP and stock market were the pinnacles of civilization. Only fools could possibly believe in something immaterial. Nevertheless, people pop SSRIs like a brighly-colored bug-eyed partier would drop X in a rural warehouse in 1991 to cope with modern living.

Television is a preferred pastime of many Westerners as a means to recharge their batteries after work. TV itself is a means to escape from reality. If the primetime shows are too much of an escape, and the scripts seem too unrealistic, there's also reality TV. TV takes a second to turn on, temporarily cures boredom, and removes the burden of having to deal with people in older-fashioned methods of curing boredom. Escaping from a stressful yet pedestrian job, where the fruits of one's labor aren't often directly enjoyed, is a testament to how shallow existence for many has become. However, their refuge from reality—TV—despite its unstimulating content, isn't a safe haven for the average Westerner given the contemptible anti-Western and politically-driven scripts that pass as "entertainment". Out of the oven and into the pan. Between a rock and a hard place. Your job sucks and your refuge hates you. Additionally, when TV doesn't quite cut it, TV airs shows filled with representations of how one should lead one's life via evoking emotions attached to affable characters, their demographic, race, sexuality, intersections, and lifestyle.

The TV spins narratives where likeable characters lead self-destructive and unsustainable lives, effortlessly balance successful careers and base debauchery. Women can become international femme fatale career women, a supermom, and a loving wife, AND be able to fit in a weekly girls' night, AND to maybe—maybe—have a raunchy affair with a swarthy blue-collar worker ten years her junior, on the side. Or, alternatively, why would you even bother having kids? They just get in the way, no? You couldn't party three times a week, make pilgrimages to party Meccas twice a year, have steamy d'alliances with exotic and sophisticated strangers while having to tend to a shrieking, pooping infant—who'll grow up to resent you anyway—now, could you? Love is besmirched. Love is cheapened. Love is debauched. Love is commodified and used as stimuli to generate sales. The traditional nuclear family unit is LAAAAAME. Hook up culture is good, actually. You too could live in a major city working forty hours a week, living in a bedsit where the rent costs the equivalent of a mortgage of a 5-bedroom in a knuckle-dragging redneck state or the country. Your thrills could also come in the form of a hoppy IPA and overpriced avocado toast. My anthropology professor told me that higher cultures enjoyed free love, boozing, and equality—why can't we? Anything in the way of my unbridled enjoyment—enjoyment which is totally authentic—is a form of liberal bourgeois oppression. I am being hampered by social constructs preventing me from achieving the utmost self-actualization. But is this who we really are? Are we little more than a socio-political experiment concocted in a university library? Have historical trends really been craftily steered in order to oppress minority groups? Should we implicitly try to emulate or absorb the characters and social dynamics televized in our favorite shows? Of course we are—this is what everyone is saying to be right, right? We can live for today, attempt to live inauthentic lives in a weak effort to appear cool to our peers. Civilization is oppressive, we can party all night, have it all, be well-rested, and still feel empowered in our quest for self-fulfillment.

Of course, this narrative isn't for everyone and doesn't apply to everyone. However, one of the worst things to come to realize is the fact that there are only 24 hours in a day; of which, for a healthy life, 1/4 to 1/3 must be earmarked for rest. For most people, they will never come to realize everything they wish to do. And, in order to get the most out of their time, sacrifices must be made. But, who, in their rightful mind, would want to make sacrifices when everybody has the potentiality to do what they want—when they want? Sacrifices require pain: the kind of pain for which there is no treatment, other than time: time which nobody wants to sacrifice. Herein lies the problem: giving up time requires self-lessness. A selfless society isn't one as willing to splash out cash for consumer goods, which is useless for an increasingly globalist economy. The only acts of selflessness that are encouraged by mainstream narratives are ones across national borders. For Westerners, acts of selflessness within the confines of one's borders would literally mean 1933 all over again, according to the media.

All of what passes as cosmopolitan trendy living can be boiled down to a certain meaninglessness for which living beyond today makes no sense if there is future financial security: your old age pension is taken care of—go enjoy, consume. Everything socially-acceptable is geared towards today. The average person is pelted with incessant advertisement, narratives, metanarratives, constantly shifting information; while given a paltry socially-approved frame of reference by the TV and their teachers, leaving them to their own devices to decode all the noise from the airwaves. Consumer goods offer sanctuary to those deprived of values greater than themselves or overwhelmed by the unrefined noise disseminated by the TV. A need to consume is omnipresent. Consumer brands offer a spiritually cheap and materially expensive means by which to ascribe oneself identity—which has, in a sense, become tacitly prohibited in polite, 'civil', society. You must refrain from partaking in identity politics as you're an individual, some say. Most identity stems from rhizomatic outgrowths of the family. Renouncing one's identity is to renounce one's sense of belonging and received meaning, as it militates against where one comes from. You are a blank slate, cut off from family. The family is the worst-offending oppressor—you won't be who you really are if you don't free yourself from their oppression. But it means to deracinate oneself; float in an abyss of relativism: unchained, unanchored, unmoored. This is to effectively kill the individual, spiritually. The concept of time won't matter within a lifespan devoid of meaning. All that matters is to fill that lifespan with vanishing experiences and consumer goods, only to get excited for the next experience or good. You cannot return to having a family to create meaning as that would be oppressive, getting in the way of your unfelt experiences.

The high time preferences exhibited by society is

reflected in one-man-one-vote democratic party politics where politicians play off the proneness to presentminded temptation of the electorate, promising them things now without drawing their attention or intelectually rationalizing the potentially negative future consequences. Politics is structured to cater short election cycles where fiscal and monetary policies can be weaponized to secure power. Instead of looking towards preserving stability or demographics, one-man-one-vote party politics with short election cycles can only operate in a society where the electorate is more presentminded. It is a self-propagating system which is destined to collapse—either through economic or demographic chaos, as a result of unsustainable short term thinking. Now, everybody can play the role of God in reshaping society to their liking. Current politics offer a facade of choice. In reality, the only choice had is to consume and vote for one of two viable candidates beholden to special interests, lobby groups, and their egos.

We're all told to live to for today, but what about the future? Well, life IS short, plus you could get hit by a bus tomorrow. YOLO. Sadly, there's always going to be some schmuck who has to pick up the tab. Thrills are cheap. Thrills are quick. But ultimately, many of the thrills enjoyed by Westerners are an escape from reality—TV, alcohol, psychoactive drugs, etc. We have socially lifted incentive structures to pursue activities and lifestyles which deny reality and offset the consequences of such a denial. It is uncool to warn others of the consequences of one's actions, especially to those imbued in a live fast, die young philosophy. Who are you to get in the way/judge me for my actions, gramps? I, too, can drink, snort, fuck till my heart's content. I won't be the one to pick up the tab when my body conks out—that's on the taxpayer. In a world where everyone is perceived to be equal, nobody is divine enough to be in a position to judge others. But sometimes, it isn't out of spite or misunderstanding as to why people may judge, but care. It is somewhat trendy to allow people to live their lives unimpeded, without instilling order or guidance. When faced with the consequences of one's actions, offering emotional protection instead of con-demnation is the socially acceptable thing to do. Many live in a constant state of infantilization, to never fully blossom into adulthood. One of the many reasons as to why so many act for today, filling their free time with meaningless and often self-deprecating experiences comes about from a total lack of self-respect, which could be a product of several reasons ranging from media propaganda to a faulty understanding of infor-mation or spirituality when forming personal value judgements. Overcoming one's impulses is a gateway to maturity. Being able to defer gratification for a greater, more appreciated, enjoyment in the future is a lost key to greater living. To derive greater fulfillment, peace of mind, and a better future, we are obliged to conquer our impulses and looking towards the future for our posterity.

To quote the old Guinness advert, "good things come to those who wait."

CHAPTER 1

WHAT ARE TIME PREFERENCES?

SIMPLY PUT, TIME PREFERENCES are how much an individual prefers present consumption over future consumption, and vice versa. Somebody is said to have a high time prefence when they'd rather consume closest to the present moment rather than in the future. Somebody is said to have a low time preference when future consumption—deferring gratification—forgoing present consumption, best suits their present needs. However, the individual in question may not be directly consuming the object for which gratification was deferred; the object or subject enjoyed may be for their children, such as an heirloom or inheritance; for a cause, such as infrastructure for a nation/community; or it may not even be tangible, such as security for their children and grandchildren. There seems to be a trend where those who appear to be more religious are keener to defer gratification into the future. This is not, to say, that for certain things they would have a low time preference; for example, food, coffee, cigarettes, etc. There are a multiplicity of objects to be consumed. For the remainder of this book, we will exclude what is deemed to be a necessity—food, water, liveable shelter—with the exception of addictive substances whose withdrawal symptoms may prove fatal. Those with high time preferences make act in a way which may harm them or their opportunities in the long term by consuming or enjoying something in the short term. Many adolescents drink, smoke, consumer recreational drugs as a form of temporary enjoyment, to ascribe status, or escape, but with potential long term health, employment, or social consequences. Some indulge in getting tattooed at a young age which they live to regret, furnishing us with an example of how high time preferences can have lasting consequences. Now, the permanent effects of tattooing can be significantly—although painfully and expensively—reduced through laser removal. During adolescence or early adulthood, the conception of time is longer. Moreover, since flying the nest, consequences and responsibility are usually assumed by one's parents instead of the child. High time preferences can alter one's life by faulty decisions made early on, thus lowering their quality of life or their reachable goals.

Time preference springs from value; in particular, how we choose to value our time and consumption while we live. Sometimes, how we choose to lead our lives or act may not be for our enjoyment, but our children's, our grandchildren's, and descendents we will never know. Time preferences may be so low as to far exceed our own life expectancies, or so high as to only seek gratification as soon as possible—regardless of the financial or social cost. It is assumed that we have shifting value scales as per the information we have at our disposal or our environment. A frequently recited illustration of value is: in a desert, after trekking for 2 days without fluids, what would you prefer when offered the simple choice between a 50 karat diamond or a bottle of water? Obviously, the offerer is exceptionally cruel to dangle something so valuable as a viable choice when the offeree is clearly parched and on death's door—and has no use for something so valuable, off this mortal coil. However, since much of today's life has been commoditized, value is almost indissolubly associated with cost. Values beyond the material are almost uncool and stupid since they'd be verging on the superstitious in polite society. The material is tangible and universally valuable according to the laws of supply and demand. The spiritual, being intangible, is impossible to assign a monetary value, especially in an increasingly globalized world/economy. Time preferences for the material, on the whole, tend to be high, and, for the spiritual, tend to be not only low, but presumably everlasting. It is no accident that in a despiritualized world, a 'living for today' outlook has reigned supreme. Everything on TV, the media, books, academia, haute societe, and the like, glorifies a high-flying life to cram as many possible experiences into your three-score-and-ten years on earth. You are to live as an atomized individual disconnected from received history, customs, spirituality, or traditions where you make your own person. You consume—and maybe produce something of marketable value to a credit-based house-of-cards economy. And even though time preferences are something linked to intelligence; if an intelligent person's values and information are presentminded, they will only be able to use their intelligence to muffle the consequences of their high time preferences rather than looking towards the future, in spite of their intelligence, and assuming that their actions are to their benefit.

Value, being subjective, can change throughout the course of the individual's life. When time is scarce, the individual may tend to be drawn towards consuming closest to the impulse identifying a will to consume such a good. Difficult to quantify, the perception of time changes throughout a person's life. When one is young, they may think they have all the time in the world. But this, of course, doesn't mean they have low time preferences. As one develops, they accumulate experiences and meld themselves according to the consequences of their actions, thus improving their ability to live their lives. Up until early adulthood, the perception of time is *long*. The consequences of their more debaucherous actions won't catch up to them yet. Jiminy Cricket begins nagging after gaining more experiences. As life passes and the person matures, there's less physical time left for them to live—obviously. However, almost paradoxically, their time preferences begin to lower, especially when facing the prospect of starting a family—the continuance of their own life after they're physically gone. Time preferences lower as there's less time to do what one needs. Unnecessary wants are filtered out by experience. Desires weaken for the consumption of material goods as values shift towards maturity. One's life force slowly dissipates after early adulthood and their will to experience and consume adjunctly dissipates, save a life-changing event such as the loss of a spouse. The future, when faced with one's own existence if one has a genetic legacy, becomes more important. Parents and grandparents will often leave their children fortunes to ensure their material comfort and security when they've passed. Through either selfishness or high time preferences, some children may not receive any inheritance after their parents have passed as the care of ensuring the material comfort or security of their children wasn't ostensibly more valuable than their enjoyment while they were still alive, illustrating how in a modern commodified society, high time preferences seem to be linked to selfishness or personal gratification. There have been recent articles toying with the idea of a confiscatory inheritance tax to fund other ends, but, if this were to ever pass, savings would decrease significantly as it would remove an incentive to lower time preferences, or, to defer gratification in the now, to fritter away those funds to other ends.

Time preferences may vary between differing ends. Sometimes, individuals may have low time preferences when it comes to their children, business, self-improvement, but when it comes to a particular eccentric outlet, their demand curve may be inelastic. suggesting a more immediate desire for that particular good. A family man with a caffeine addiction might need a cup of coffee to be more agreeable to his family in the morning: marching straight to the kitchen with his head down for a cup of Joe before properly addressing anyone, for example. For certain things, time preferences may be high, and for others, low. However, the purpose of this short book isn't to split hairs, but to attempt to illustrate how one's general outlook on the question of apportioning one's time—especially when it comes to values greater than oneself. If one makes themself their highest value by elevating themself above all else through either a predisposition to egoism or solipsism, their perception of time ends with them. They will have, on the whole, high time preferences to enjoy and consume. Low time preferences, if the person in question doesn't have children as an extension of life beyond their own, would be considerably shorter as gratification is assumed to be enjoyed within their own life expectancy. Gratification begins and ends with them and their time horizons would be significantly shorter, even if they were more future-oriented.

One of the many sicknesses in Western society has been the increasing meaningless of time. Time has lost meaning, as time, being a portion of one's life, has been affected by the loss in self-respect which has been glorified through self-destructive trendy pseudophilosophies, consumerism, and pitifully demanding respect from others to compensate for a lack of their own. Time has meaning, but that meaning has been obscured by the material and the will to gratify oneself. In a race to the bottom, time is simply an obstacle, a fetter, to achieving maximum consumption. Selfishness is running riot, the awareness of one's physical time heightens the want to reach gratification, raising time preferences. As part of the normalization of selfishness, there have been demands to further liberalize society in the name of freedom—freedom from oppression—but in reality, what's more demanded, is a will to free oneself from oneself; to become something that they're not; to transcend one's unassailable limits. But, as there are limits to one's abilities, they need to run a race to the bottom, to will to become oppressed as society will confer them more freedom, thus making the individual wish to become further oppressed as in many circles steeped in social justice theory, being 'oppressed' grants status without exerting effort. Naturally, individuals respond to incentive structures and seek status, as being social animals. If one is socially rewarded for certain behaviors, they will act accordingly. The desire to free oneself from oneself, due to an odium for the deficiencies of one's self-image through propagandizing and perverse incentive structures, creates a will for inauthenticity propped up by the prevailing narratives, leading to an abject lack of self-respect or meaning. The meaningless of time is a by-product of the perceived meaningless of one's life, which many desperately attempt to plaster over with consumer goods and entertainment which belong to a certain brand, which offer a form of identification.

Physical Time

How everyone as a whole experiences time, recognized measured time, or how much time one will live ie. life expectancy.

Perceived Time

How much time an individual reckons they have to complete a task. When having fun, time goes quickly. When bored, time runs slowly. Physical time continues to run in spite of how much fun or boredom the individual is having. When perceived time is long, such as in early adulthood, time preferences are high as consequences are farther away, except when one believes in eternal life, as there will be judgement for one's worldly actions.

As time preference is subjective, it is, therefore, difficult to quantify or measure. An individual's time preference constantly shifts as per their present requirements, interests, knowledge, financial situation, marital status, children and throughout one's life and maturity. Time preferences for different ends and values may change. There are many factors which will influence how one perceives time or how gratification will be valorized. Depending if the individual in question is endowed with intelligence—maturity, in particular—will that individual tend to act more towards the future. If one's immediate environment is chaotic, it follows that time preferences will be high as there is too much change and instability, preventing one from formulating calculated long-sighted decisions into the future as meanings extrinsic to the individual in question could differ between two given points in time. If there's order, stability, and values in place which are greater than the individual, then social time preferences will be low and social pressures will be calibrated to weed out high time preferences and low impulse control as they jeopardize the integrity of such a social arrangement. Low time preferences presuppose the society as to outlive the individual and as something worth preserving. If the society's preservation becomes devalued through sustained propagandizing, negatively portraying it as intrinsically evil, then time preferences will be high has the group will feel disconnected to that society and have lower self-confidence for being part of such a great evil. Living for today—and only today—is a renunciation of the future. It indicates a thorough lack of self-respect and rootlessness, blowing in the winds of change to settle wherever one may land. And one has begun to yearn constant change to inflate oneself with meaning. When everything becomes subjective, time becomes distorted. One can monetize their own time by offering their services as a means by which they can assign value to their own self-worth. 'My time is worth X amount per hour' says the lawyer, financial advisor, and sales rep. In assigning a monetary value to time, the less inclined many will become to hand out their scarce free time to others and prefer to keep it for oneself, as time is a portion of one's life.

Why is It Important?

Given that 'life is short', and there are only 24 hours a day, time preferences dictate much of our lives: who we spend time with, who we marry (assuming that marriage is for life), our employment, where we live, our hobbies, etc. Without being able to calculate how much time must be given to the utmost ends, life becomes disorganized and impulsive. How much one values intangible or immaterial things may be related to lower time preferences. Money comes and goes—and there are certain things money can't buy. A more materialistic life appears to be more impulsive, on the whole. To make lucrative investments, intelligence is required. An impulsive financial manager or investor isn't often a very successful one. For most, low time preferences don't come naturally. There must be a reason for them to wish to be more future-oriented. There needs to be something to prompt them to radically alter their incentive structures and value scales in spite of social mores. That something is usually children. That's not to say, however, that children are the be all and end all of lower time preferences. We're often treated, by the tabloid press, to many stories of drug-addicted parents who neglect their child in favor of dosing themselves. For some, the incentive behind having children is to increase their social parasitism in the form of larger welfare checks. Others are simply indifferent to their children or view them as an obstacle to their material enjoyment. Assuming that we wish to preserve some semblance of civilization, it is imperative that incentive structures be rearranged with the goal to reinforce the best behaviors, morals, and values. Social trust deteriorates in the face of impulsiveness. Revamping the concept of bread and circuses under the pretense of instilling social passivity will cause long-lasting, if not, irreparable consequences. High time preferences and presentmindedness associate themselves with a decivilizing selfishness hazardous to the preservation of a long-lasting social formation. The importance of understanding consequences to one's actions is paramount to responsibility and duty—both of which have been lost under a miasma of trendy verbiage and celebrated social policies. The types of work and social ethics birthed by such gross social negligence mark a return to barbarism. Entitlement culture is real. Entitlement is a privileged form of high time preferences. It denotes a fundamental lack of respect to one's peers and a desertion of discipline. Individuals have been bounteously pampered by unrivalled luxury and trendy social mantras—plus there are little to no social consequences to being entitled. Why would somebody take the time to be patient or understanding if nothing happens as a consequence to their poor manners? Like a two-year-old experimenting their social boundaries by acting outrageously only to throw a tantrum when castigated by their parents— supposing they have two loving parents—many young adults live in a similar state of childishness. A two-year-old doesn't know any better. This is why adults impose boundaries: to mould a human being fit to become an integrated and active member of society. It would be fundamentally ruinous to a child to fail to impose boundaries and rules. We often see spoilt children where the parent(s) fail to discipline the child after each reckless impulse; unfortunately, we see a similar spectacle with many young adults who are tremendously unfit to be termed "adult". There's no need for them to practice discipline as there are no consequences. In fact, their lack of discipline is often praised by their peers and the media. What happens when they have children? Will they automatically become endowed with wisdom and discipline to impart to their children? I sincerely doubt it. What of the next generation if they—the undisciplined, the entitled—are to be their progenitors? Perhaps, the awesome growth of technology may keep society together like a titanium linchpin. Perhaps, fully automated luxury gay space communism may be the answer to our post-societal prayers. Unless we were to achieve something similar to post-scarcity in order to satiate the impulsive demands of all, I personally cannot see this anomalous social experiment—western civilization—surviving in a few generations. Several writers dating back as far as the early second-half of the 19th century prophesied the West's fall into nihilism and decadence. Historians in the first half of the 20th century put forward a cyclical theory of civilization. The final stages of civilization are generally marked by frivolous and materialistic activities—seemingly to keep boredom at bay. Duty disappears, responsibility retreats, capital consumption outpaces net productivity, the consequences of one's actions are socialized, and incentive structures in place disincentivize sacrifice.

One of the many modern truisms is that "life is short"; therefore, as many experiences must be accumulated to constitute a life well lived. However, there is one simple trick to extend life beyond one's own short span: children. Some may consider this to be "party pooping". When information or situations change, value scales change. When somebody is in their early adulthood, many wish to start a family in their 30s—they would be burnt out from partying and sleeping around, they will have accumulated resources, and matured a little more. Children would be an impediment to that lifestyle. In early adulthood, after being unshackled from the constraints of living under the roof of one's parent(s), they experience an unparalleled freedom; a rebirth, so to speak. Their perception of physical time is long. There is time to do whatever one wants before settling down. There is time to gain new experiences and to "find oneself" after being released from the strictures of their oppressive parent(s). This life fast, die young mentality wishes to extend itself as far as possible into one's life. Living fast and dying young is a plea for help. It has become cool to live fast and die young. This form of lifestyle is something to aspire to. It is all over the TV. It is encouraged by parents and cool wine aunts alike. There are no consequences to living in such a way, and, if there are, you'll be old—that's for future 'you' to worry about. After the philosophical death of God, as there is no judgement after death: anything goes. And a higher time preference implies a greater willingness for immediate completion or satiety, calling for a quicker termination of the life cycle of a certain process. A higher time preference also implies a will to bring about an end as one's perception of their own life is short. The 'live fast, die young' credo epitomizes the high time preference mentality.

Returning back to John Lennon's Imagine, what would happen if everyone were to be "living for today"? Who'd worry about tomorrow? Somebody has to. Our children will pick up the tab for our actions, if we're not too careful. If we consumed like locusts, what will be left after we're gone—and I'm not just talking about consumption in general, what of the nations our ancestors built: the architecture, the art, the culture, the blood shed, the lives lost, the turmoil, strife, and hardship endured so that we could enjoy a safe and luxurious (decaying) civilization? It's not too hard to imagine— we're seeing its decline in real time. Rome declined gradually for around 10-15 generations before it eventually fell. The West is in an uncannily similar process of decline, perhaps accelerated by the accessibility of technology and unprecedented levels of wealth creation which sedates the individual from the realization many social ills. Consumerism blinkers the individual from distress. Almost like a local anaesthetic, that needs to be constantly reapplied to dull the pain of modern life; people don't want to look up from the consumerist feeding trough to see the impending dangers wrought by their selfish, self-deifying, vapid lifestyles. Many may see the problems conceived by their passivity and selfishness, but figure they'll be six-foot under by the time their chickens come home to roost. Their lives burn up quicker than a shooting star, and, like a shooting star, their memory will enjoy a similar lifespan. They wish not to suffer the consequences of their actions, avoiding guilt by materialist distractions, which, in turn, sets in motion a decivilizing piranha-like voracity to satiate their multiple galloping desires. And in a similar piranha-like fashion, those who purely live by high time preferences relegate their behaviors to something more animal, primitive, carnal, rather than civil.

Presently, there are many conditions and incentive

structures in place where our decision-making has become presentminded and selfish. Discipline—which is a fundamental element to having a low time prefence— is atavistic, unglamorous, and unnecessary to many given how incentive structures are shaped to exclude the need for discipline or sacrifice. Discipline and sacrifice alike are painful and burdensome in an age where technology, science, and the State can be commanded to better the human condition, and to render exertion a thing of the past. High time preferences stimulated by our incentive structures have rendered the qualities invaluable to creating civilization or a healthy society a thing of the past. In fact, the opposite is happening: currently decivilizing incentive structures reward presentmindedness and offset the consequences onto those with, on the whole, low time preferences—such as middle class taxpayers. Although lacking explicitness, it seems fairly clear as to what ends many tax dollars serve, thus raising time preferences of those middle class taxpayers, seeing a certain meaningless and futility in living for tomorrow if their efforts will go towards the indolent today.

You get the government you deserve, and, by extension, the global economic policy—neoliberalism—too. The current situation is a consequence of high time preferences, and a wilful abandonment of higher values which obstructed immediate gratification and defanged the sense of guilt which is brought about by the abandonment of such higher values. Higher values, often associated with religiosity, are devalued by the availability of replacement, such as consumer goods.

Environments with higher levels of stress tend to produce greater levels of religiosity. Consumer goods, recreational drugs, prescription drugs, media narratives, and several things at our disposal reduce the stress of socially high time preferences without the need for a rediscovery of more spiritually-satifying values.

How we organize our use of physical time to ensure the safest navigation of our actions for the best ends and to lessen negative consequences is optimal to preserving a healthy society in the face of change or adversity. What happens when everyone acts in their own self interest when thinking for tomorrow isn't an option? The fat of the land is trimmed. What's left for tomorrow? Nothing. Fuck tomorrow. That's a problem for somebody else's kids—the ones who are coming to supposedly pay for our state pensions as we didn't have kids of our own because we were out being empowered/having fun instead.

The Metaphysics of Time Preferences

What is the point of deferring gratification?

The default position for most is to have a low impulse control, i.e. high time preferences. Without choices or an incentive structure in place to make succumbing to one's impulses less desirable; most individuals, without good reason, would prefer to enjoy something pleasurable immediately rather than having to wait. Something situational or environmental must take place in order for individuals to need to lower their time preferences in the form of an incentive structure. If food or resources are abundant, there's no real reason to have low time preferences as everything germain to survival is omnipresent and extraordinary measures necessary to maintain survival are redundant. Conversely, if food and/or resources are scant, choices and incentive structures change to accommodate for a more hostile environment. Those less able to use foresight or deferral of gratification die out, given the hostile living conditions. They, sadly for them, miss the opportunity to pass on their genes onto the subsequent generation, excluding less adept survivors to these hostile living conditions. Over time, behaviors skewed to having high time preferences are weeded out by nature.

Drivers in approaching lower time preferences can be split into two categories:

1) Tangible

Monetary and material reasons to become more future-oriented such as an investment, purchasing a house, a business, etc.

2) Intangible

Spiritual, familial, and personal reasons beyond the material to lower time preferences such as religiosity, having a child, or self-improvement for a physically/mentally demanding event, etc.

There are certain uncomfortable factors—discipline, responsibility, duty, consequence, and sacrifice—which need to overvalue immediate comfort and gratification, in order to have low time preferences. Time preferences tend to be expressed in gratification or consumption, often manifesting in a material transaction.

Furthermore, reproductive strategies vis-a-vis living conditions emerge. This has often been controversially referred to as r/K selection theory: r-selection denotes: high time preferences, promiscuity, low parental investment strategy, higher rates of twin-births, narrower hips & birth canals, early puberty, stronger muscles in males, shorter menstrual cycles, more children overall, smaller baby skull size.

K-selection denotes:

- less children
- high parental investment strategy
- low time preferences
- highly territorial
- later puberty
- weaker muscles
- longer menstrual cycles
- larger baby skull size
- less twins

Humans can exhibit traits of both r and K selection, and, as a theory, humans rest on a spectrum between both extremes. However, given human biodiversity, I am attempting to illustrate how certain individuals are disposed to different incentive structures on the subject of time preferences. Most crucially, parental investment strategy is strongly associated to time preferences. A low investment parental strategy in a harsh climate reliant on scant resources and seasonal food sources would spell extinction for that particular community. A high-investment parental strategy wouldn't be as necessary in an environment with abundant food sources or resources. In such an environment a higher rate of infant mortality than in a harsher climate wouldn't be as detrimental to the survival of the group. Long term decision making is less of an imperative in environments blessed with food or resources as food production rarely becomes a concern—absent a freak natural event.

Sophisticated methods of agriculture aren't necessary. Agriculture requires low time preferences. Farming with high time preferences or low impulse control would be a free-for-all. Ploughed fields would return to a state of nature very shortly after the abandonment of such practices. And for K-selected parental investment strategies to flourish, there needs to exist a semblance of social stability, otherwise, a K-selected parental investment strategy would prove thoroughly impractical, as attention in raising fewer children would be reduced because of everpresent social chaos.

There has to be a reason to wanting to avoid pleasure in the here and now—and that would be for a greater pleasure in the future. Peace of mind for posterity, enjoying the benefits from a well-calculated investment, closer communion with a deity, etc: would all constitute a greater—and more lasting—pleasure than immediate consumption with a fleeting reward. Eventually, the fleeting reward evaporates and new rewards must be sought out to stimulate the individual.

The energy is lost over time. The lifeforce which yields pleasure in a certain activity or consumption dwindles. Even an energy tapped from the divine can wane over time. Nevertheless, this energy, although loses motivation over time, usually wanes as a result of the actions of selfish people using the divine to serve their own material or political ends. Its support and inspiration loses vigor, when the original purpose or message is debased.

An enjoyable task can become repetitive and boring. Boredom is an absence of stimuli. For example, many individuals who have been married for a while complain that sex—something enjoyable to most—becomes stale and have to, therefore, 'spice things up'; in other words, try something new to give a sense of stimulation: energy.

When this energy is sapped, it is difficult to rekindle the flame without deauthenticating the original message. For example, protestant countries boast far higher rates of atheism than countries which remained primarily Catholic after the Reformation. But this transition into atheism in Protestant countries, like a slow-boiled frog, was a long process which saw a remarkably hurried death.

The same applies with the idea of the nation or family. If theres a neverending onslaught of information fired at the nation or family, belief in those values will wane as individuals become demoralized. Divorce rates are on the up and the number of individuals willing to make the ultimate sacrifice are at a record low. However, when presented with an imminent threat without neverending toxic propaganda devalorizing, when conscious of its fate as a nation or family, its energy is smacked with a jab of adrenaline to deal with the existential threat. In the winter of civilization, a recrudescence of energy in the form of romantic nationalism—a belief in an end greater than oneself, which can be perceived as secular—is apparent as that society becomes conscious of its looming end. At this stage, there seems to be a bifurcation of transcendental ends: one placing its highest ends something greater than itself, and the other, elevating oneself into the highest value, thus limiting the highest value to the deification of oneself.

Will power can be understood as to tame one's impulses. It takes will power to quit smoking or lose weight which require being able to tame one's impulses for a long term gain.

With a goal in mind for one's future benefit, impulses can be successfully staved off for the betterment of the individual. But before the will is to be mastered, there has to be a reason to do so. When social, economic, and political incentive structures in such a way to reward impulsiveness and punish discipline; it doesn't take much to figure out what the final result will be. There is no reason to have low time preferences. At the end stage of a civilization where its history is reviled, its people demonized, alternative impulsive pseudo-philosophies occupy the valueless void, state handouts are used to impulsive ends, entertainment is omnipresent as an escape, jobs are meaningless and soul-destroying, money is debased, neighborhoods change in front of their residents' very eyes: why would anybody look towards deferring their gratification beyond their own lives if there isn't much for their children to inherit? It seems that the crippling lack of the presence of something greater than one's very life has seen much spare time frittered away to empty ends.

CHAPTER 2

THE WILL-TO-GRATIFICATION

As WE TRUDGE ONWARDS to a neoliberal post-industrial utopia, the phrase 'low impulse control' doesn't quite cut it when most desires are commodified marketable goods. A new phrase adopting old terms is in order. Something which sounds pre-eminent is needed to describe the insatiable urge for constant gratification in the void excavated in our hearts by the loss of a certain joie de vivre. Low impulse control implies less licit methods in scratching the materialist itch. No, we keep it kosher. We exchange tender for our goods. We have the money—we just want the goods. If we simply had low impulse control, we'd be shop lifting and looting to sate our material needs. What we yearn for is a non-descript material good to ascribe us some meaning and diversion. But we can't wait for the next iPhone or handheld console. Let us all just go apeshit, forming block-long queues, and let our bearded jaws hit the floor when proudly snapping selfies next to our latest product for our social media followers. This is how steam is blown off and our perception of time can be manipulated to make way for the next cool gadget or handheld console.

High time preferences in a civilized milieu can be

described as a will-to-gratification. This will doesn't factor in future costs, opportunity costs—both social and financial—and seeks to gratify the consumer at the nearest possible opportunity. High time preferences can also be perceived as being selfish, and, while high time preferences can be for selfless ends such as a charity alleviating poverty in a downtrodden area, it usually isn't in the best interest of the person at hand to make rash decisions. Rushing into decision-making concerning gratification is risky business—especially when certain decisions have far-reaching consequences. Every Western government has overburdened their taxpayer, piled on their national debts, engaged in irresponsible spending, expanded like a Californian wildfire, and are on the brink of insolvency. Why? Mostly due to gratifying the electorate and politician alike. Where there is universal suffrage, if the electorate is presentminded (has high time preferences), we will invariably witness a meteoric rise in the size of its debts, currency debasement, and social programs. Sadly, somebody's gotta pay for it, but that fact is furtively swept under the rug when these policies are triumphantly unveiled. That somebody is a future generation under the leadership of a politician, who, the original electorate would find unpalatably ghastly. The politicians who enjoyed their time in office riding on a ticket of social programs are either out of office or six feet under. In the long run, we're all dead.

The natural state of people, on the whole, isn't to defer gratification. There needs to be a reason to think about the future—an incentive structure. Since the modern era, the Industrial Revolution, and the wealth created by latter, hardship is slowly but surely becoming a thing of the past. Questions concerning the incentive structures attached to a materially better off society must be asked. Everything is in place for us to not only avoid hardship like the plague, but also to stimulate our will-to-gratification. Consumption is, not only socially encouraged, but also assisted by short-term finance and diversified by the overwhelming choice of consumer products at our disposal.

This isn't, to say, a call to avoid gratification altogether, but an invitation to rethink how gratification is earned. For example, purchasing an exotic holiday without the use of a credit card or a short-term loan may require months of saving and tightening-of-the-belt in order for it to become affordable. With either a credit card or a short-term loan, that exotic holiday can become yours without much of an afterthough—that is, until, of course, you come home from your holiday, but, hey! At least you'd have had peace of mind for like, a week or so. Cutting corners is part of our nature. To take the long way round is foolish when there are shortcuts a-plenty.

The will-to-gratification is also followed by a denial of reality. This denial of reality could simply start with living outside one's financial means or end with the fiscal feasability of a State pension scheme. One's will-to-gratification could lead somebody to deny other forms of realities, such as a will to gratify one's yearning for a pizza—telling oneself that they'll burn it off at the gym tomorrow. It takes wisdom to know that you probably won't hit the gym. It takes sacrifice in opting for a salad instead. But the end result is a taut and more attractive figure in the long run which could lead you to harvest a greater happiness, such as, attracting a spouse you might not have done as a tub of lard; let alone falling into a rut of gratification. Eg: I had a pizza last weekend, fuck it, it was delicious, I'll have one tonight too. Additionally, you're beautiful/healthy at any size and if somebody criticizes your girth with mirth, tell them how bigoted and backwards they are.

Many of the decisions we make in satisfying our wants—gratifying ourselves—may be subconscious or almost second nature, habit. Opting to draw the credit card from your pocket for something you burningly desire with greater swift and dexterity than a six-shooter from a cowboy's holster has, in many instances, become instinctive. Without presently holding the necessary funds, it's not the end of the world, the new debt you've accrued for gratification may mean having to rein it in a little afterwards.

In some instances, the will-to-grafitication could be viewed as a crude medium to banish one's lack of self-respect. Incautiously consuming without, at least, considering the side-effects to gratification indicates a lack of self-respect. A self-respecting individual would not pile on debt—and the pounds—for cheap thrills or gratification with a shorter lifespan than a twinkling in one's eye. And herein lies the problem: many individuals abjectly lack self-respect. They saddle themselves with debt; they allow their waistlines to balloon up; they lose friends/ relationships/marriages. Partly due to a lack of self-respect which characterizes the will-to-gratification. Instead of reconciling one's differences, it's sometimes easier divorce. But, what about the kids? They'll be ok.

This lack of self-respect has cropped up from a variety of reasons which I explore in later chapters. The lack of respect is the coal to the will-to-gratification; the social incentive structure maternally empathazing with one's weaknesses, its oxygen; the Narrative Complex's cheerleading from the sidelines, its bellow; unbacked currency and the easy availability of short-term loans/credit, its lighter fuel.

There's an episode of the Simpsons where Homer says, "that's for future Homer". The future is yet to reveal itself and I'll deal with the consequences then, even if they're worse than what I'd have to deal with now—the point is: it doesn't have to be dealt with now. Consumption and enjoyment can be experienced now. Those undesirable consequences rearing their ugly head down the timeline won't be felt quite yet. There is a distinction before low time preferences and being laid back. Spaniards are famed for their siesta culture, indulging in nap times and deferring responsibility for another day—often, 'mañana'. But, in this case, gratification comes in being temporarily care-free and not having to bear the unpleasantness of taking responsibility or fulfilling an undesirable task. Being laid back can be perceived as having high time preferences as doing nothing is more valuable to the individual or group than productivity. Mañana is yet to come. Perhaps the responsibility-laden siesta aficionado may feel as if they're in a better position to execute their responsibilities another time, at their next convenience, or simply hope that their problems evaporate into thin air.

One could go a step further and suggest the will-to-gratification to be a modernized version of the Pleasure Principle. One strives to acquire as much pleasure, in the forms of frivolous material goods/experiences, but to never come down from the high of enjoyment. Pleasure is often selfish, failing to take others into consideration. High time preferences with the basic use of the Id and Ego reveals itself as low impulse control as social norms and prevailing morality dictates these behaviors as unwanted: crime, thefts, violence, sexual assault, etc, for the immediate gratification of the pleasure seeker. Incorporating the Superego to navigate complex social norms and prevailing morality for one's immediate gratification is the will-to-gratification as it understands certain repercussions in committing crimes, such as the loss of freedom to gratify oneself in the future if caught committing said crimes. However, this does not preclude the existence of more sophisticated crimes. What I attempt to illustrate here is the will-to-gratification, although under the banner of high time preferences, is separate from simple low impulse control as it is cognizant of repercussions which may hamper its ability to gratify in the future. While immediate gratification is the name of the game, future potential gratification with new experiences cannot be limited either as it seeks to protect itself from social situations reducing the potentiality for gratification. Low impulse control for one's immediate gratification may, indeed, limit the physical time for gratification down the timeline, but it is a rawer, more primordial, method of achieving one's own ends. High time preferences, on the whole, demonstrate selfishness for one's own pleasure, with the exception of somebody in financial turmoil, for example, who lives paycheck-to-paycheck to feed themself or their children. But in this case, a higher purpose is at stake: their child's life or their own, qualifying as survival mode rather than gratification.

The will-to-gratification is a rarified method by which one can cram as much gratification into their physical time as possible. The will-to-gratification is inherently selfish. The need for altruism, in many cases, has been taken care of by the introduction of ample social programs. Economic systems are designed to maximize profit, productivity, and consumption. So, what's left other than to gratify oneself? Values shift towards material gratification instead of other more spiritual ends. Our time on Earth is short, so why not simply go nuts? Become a consuming-producer. Gratify yourself.

CHAPTER 3

INCENTIVE STRUCTURES

THE PURPOSE OF THIS SHORT BOOK is not to hold a debate between free will and determinism. However, an important recurring theme in evaluating time preferences is to address the existing incentive structures in place which could influence the choices made individually, collectively, and politically. Everybody consumes: without consumption, there couldn't be life. Simple as. With the unprecedented levels of wealth enjoyed in Western countries, the average Joe is overwhelmed by choice and choices. Deferring gratification becomes an afterthought. Immediately, this incentive structure indicates that waiting to consume is only constrained by store opening hours—except that internet shopping is 24 hours a day and high street stores are quickly becoming a relic.

Not only do incentive structures influence choice, but can also represent a lopsided version of reality, obfuscating the choices at hand. Information constructing our realities also influence what we perceive to be our incentive structures. Believing in a set of choices to be optimal despite negative potential consequences—for example, drinking and whoring—because social norms have warmed up to these ideas, also comprise part of our incentive structures. Information pumped out by various institutions may alter our incentive structures to our detriment. Likewise, certain economic policies and social programs may alter the way we view how gratification to be earned and when to be received. With the Information Complex sycophantically defending external changes to our incentive structure, such as the aforementioned change in economic policies or social programs, we are to believe that this change is both necessary and beneficial.

Soft Change to Incentive Structure

This change to our incentive structures come from within—our experiences, values, information, and perception of reality. Of course, a soft change to our incentive structure can occur through faulty or incomplete information. We may rearrange our lives according to a shift in information such as changes in social norms or in what we believe. Soft changes may come about by age and changes in interests, for example liking rap at 13, classic rock at 23, and classical music at 33. Soft changes come about through differing information or socio-cultural trends as one lives their life.

Hard Change to Incentive Structure

Incentive structures may alter according to physical external changes such as a change in economic policies, having a child, a change in marital status, or big events directly impacting one's life outside of their control. Hard changes to incentive structures are usually in the form of an imposition on one's life, forcing an adequate adjustment to what gratifies them.

In the preceding chapter, I mentioned two brief hypothetical scenarios involving two forms of gratification deferral: the first required money; the second, food.

1) Situation: Work is kicking my ass. I have $2500 in the bank. Need a vacation.

What is desired: Exotic holiday to Tahiti

Choices:
- Exotic Holiday to Tahiti $5000
- Holiday at more modest resort $1500
- Staying put $0

Value scale:
(if credit isn't available)
- Holiday at more modest resort $1500
- Exotic Holiday to Tahiti $5000
- Staying put $0

(if credit is available)
- Exotic Holiday to Tahiti $5000
- Holiday at more modest resort $1500
- Staying put $0

Social:
Your friends and family encourage you to treat yourself.

Life's short, so what are you waiting for? It would be a fabulous experience. You can brag to all your friends about what a wonderful time you had. You could also make them jealous in the process by posting photos of soft white sand, turquoise seas, and attractive members of the opposite sex you've befriended. Nobody wants to tell you that your money could be better spent or that you're living outside your means in the present.

Future Cost/sacrifice:

Provided the individual in question has access to credit in order to pay for the exotic vacation, the sacrifice or future cost of their vacation will be absorbed in future monthly payments. No a priori sacrifice is needed to be made before embarking on their vacation. The incentive structure in place isn't a structure per se, but the opposite. The incentive structure disassembles any structure preventing individuals from reaching their material goals. Anything obstructions from one's immediate happiness must be blazed from the trail—within reason. As a result, one's perception of the future becomes distorted and impaired. Inaccurate information coupled with incentive structures removing any resistance to people's material happiness render more future oriented ends less valuable. Having financial crutches—credit cards, short term loans, cash advances, etc—at one's disposal devalues future ends, and have individuals living more in the present.

2) Situation: had a rough week, hungry, socializing with friends

What is desired: Family-size pizza, chicken wings, mozzarella sticks, and a diet cola.

Choices:
(Assuming monetary cost isn't an issue)
-   Family size pizza & trimmings
-   A more modest meal
-   A salad

Value scale:
-   Family size pizza & trimmings
-   A more modest meal
-   A salad

Social:
You may pile on a few pounds if your burgeoning eating habits snowball into a lardy avalanche, but it isn't your fault You can hit the gym later. You can eat a salad later. This kind of future possibility is more appetizing when you're salivating over the prospect of a pizza pie in the now. Your friends may feel reluctant to draw your midriff to your attention—who wants the drama? In the age of hyperinclusivity, your poor choices have to be socially accepted. This form of enabling is a bizarre form of indifference; an active indifference masquerading as a social philosophy—one where individuals ignore consequences as a means of avoiding them.

Future Cost:

You'll feel less athletic, attractive, agile, healthy, and confident. Obesity costs the UK taxpayer $42bn a year. You may not be able to attract a partner you may have done when you were thinner, thus lowering your future quality of life.

Sacrifice:

Some pleasures need to be nipped in the bud. While a large pizza may feel satisfying, tantalizingly tingling your tastebuds now, you'll feel dehydrated and sluggish later. Falling into a groove of binging on anything, not just food, is very easy to do. The immediate pleasure from binging on X outweighs its negative side-effects. Values change to reflect a predilection for X (pizza in this case) while ignoring the immediate, but accumulative, negative side-effects which could amount to unwanted ailments. Forgoing pizza, in this case, and sticking to a more boring exercise and diet regimen could amount to greater satisfaction: having a good physique, attracting a high quality sexual partner, longevity, disease prevention, physical fitness, greater drive/motivation, job promotion, etc.

In both hypothetical situations, the incentive "structure" removes consequences and promotes vice to maximize material pleasure. What we have is a form of epicureanism on a cocktail of cocaine, meth, and trenbolone where consequences to one's actions have been merely concealed, and not fully removed. Consequences will materialize in the future, but, as I've previously stated, the ability to conceptualize future ends—both positive or negative—has been impaired and devalued, and is therefore, to be ignored for its awkwardness.

Reward:

Reward is key to an incentive structure. Why would one value a certain end in itself if it derives no reward? In forming complex interrelations with individuals, Game Theory can be used to conceptually understand how one can achieve an optimal pay off.

When arriving at a certain fork in the road, people will tend to take the path of least resistance when proceeding. When evaluating opportunity cost, the end goal/product envisaged hasn't yet materialized, and therefore, does not exist. It is, therefore, something to be taken into consideration when striving towards something that doesn't materially exist—a disincentive. The path of least resistance can be seen as a disutility for labor—assuming labor is painful/undesirable to the individual as he isn't a workaholic.

Going forward, we will examine the incentive structure in place for certain occurrences plaguing Western society. The incentive structures in place should assist in elucidating as to why certain occurrences have hitherto been so detrimental to Western society; how present-mindedness instead of a future-oriented, gratification-deferring view to the future has unleashed our consumerist hellscape. A loss of a future beyond ones own life denotes a loss in a belief greater than oneself. Man becomes the measure of all things.

Amygdala

An interesting phrase, which has recently lost popularity, is 'to activate one's almonds'—almonds being a
metaphor for one's amygdala. In actual fact, the word
amygdala is derived from almond. The function of the
amygdala is to give the mind a certain feeling of danger
to protect the individual from harm. For example, that
nagging feeling that makes you reconsider pulling off a
'hold-my-beer' tier daredevil stunt is your amygdala. It
grows with experience. A toddler doesn't know it's a
bad idea to stick its fingers in a power socket, but an
adult does. The amygdala allows one to perceive threats
and to avoid actions why may prove later harmful.
Rodents which have had their amygdala removed will
snuggle up to a cat—a predator. Nothing compels them
to disperse for their lives' sake. Under our current
standards and alternative methods in child-rearing,
especially one's that neglect discipline in favor of some
wishy washy gobbledygook; people are being raised free
from consequences. Superficially, it may sound kind and
lovely, but a great disservice is being done to them as
they are raised to be thoroughly ill-equipped for the real
world. Acting on impulse and immediate gratification,
without much notable consequence, is tremendously
destructive to somebody's formation. What kind of a
message is conveyed to children who are handed a
participation trophy for coming in last? Participation
trophies are most often handed to save the feelings of
children. Failure is rewarded. One can gain social status
by pretending to being emotionally hurt, playing the
victim, and claiming offence. Society will bend over

backwards to comfort them. Now we have a hierarchical inversion—those who have been most ostensibly wronged by western society must be artificially elevated to the highest echelons in the name of social justice.

Other behavioral traits have been linked to having atrophied amygdala, including: envy, resentment, disdain for competition, entitlement, and a rejection of hierarchy.

An incentive structure where competition and adrenaline-pumping experiences are minimized, effectually bubble-wrapping individuals may also have unintended psychological consequences. The way to hell is paved with good intentions and much of this social bubble-wrapping has been introduced WITH good intentions, but dire consequences—consequences which our bubble-wrapping won't be able to soften the blow of reality, when that day finally comes.

Some, not all, have been raised in an environment of unreality who have a considerable amount of influence in political decision-making. Many were born with a silver spoon in their mouths and have been fasttracked through prestigious schools and universities into handsome careers. Sadly, despite their influence, they have very limited interraction with the real world. In America, at least, this demographic lives on the coast, probably in likeminded homogeneous communities. They witness a changing world, which they enthusiastically welcome. Some of the policies they'd wish to enact would mount considerable pressure on the rest of the country, but their former professor, who writes a scintillating column for a mainstream coastal publication assures them that this is desirable: this is progress. People of other backgrounds they come into contact with are highly-educated, likeminded, and have been fully assimilated into western values. They form opinions surrounding their lived experience, the views of their contemporaries—often regurgitated talking points from the mainstream intelligentsia—and the mainstream media. To drift off their intellectual reservation could spell trouble for their social standing. Ostracism would be their social death sentence. As a result of living in such a safe environment, having their flow of information restricted to establishment-approved sources and lapdogs; they know not what they do in some of their policies as their perception of reality is incomplete at best, false at worst. Like the rodent who snuggles up to the cat, some of the policies in which they believe are forms of demographic suicide.

The incentive structure here is belonging. Believing in things which may not be in one's best interest, to the outsider, may appear to be absurd. But, if their reality has been distorted by false information and a reward in the form of a dopamine hit everytime one virtue signals is earned, then it's easier to enjoy the immediate gratification of the dopamine hit and to avoid the pain of social exclusion and a tacit loss of identity.

Maslow Hierarchy of Needs

From top to bottom:

- Self actualization: to fulfill one's highest potential in line with their desires

- Esteem: to be filled with confidence, status, and conscious of one's station in life
- Love and Belonging: to have friends, family, intimacy, higher bonds.
- Safety: to have security in one's source of funds, person, and livelihood
- Physiological Needs: to have food, shelter, warmth

As we can judge from Maslow's hierarchy of needs, many glum individuals in question enjoy the bottom two needs in abundance. The top three needs have become commodified and reified to include prevailing social norms. Families have been torn apart, friendships are often reliant on being a representation of what one is expected to be rather than oneself, confidence has been ripped asunder through Narrative Complex propagandizing, the tall poppy must be cut down, and self-actualization is unreachable in many cases as the narrative dictates that one's potentiality is both beyond one's own and inauthentic. It's like you're always stuck in second gear. Life is reduced to the two lowest needs. Why aim higher?

From 2015 onwards there has been a migrant crisis originally stemming from the War in Syria and the political left after the gung-ho removal of Muammar Gaddafi in Libya. Consequently, millions have been displaced in the Middle East and open air slave markets freely trade Africans in Libya. The were reports that with the initial movements from the Middle East to Europe, several non-Syrian opportunists had used the catastrophe as a means to tailgate into Europe in order to exploit their generous welfare payments or to be reunified with their families who were already living there. Between 2-3% of those who cross the Mediterranean from Africa into Europe drown. But why would people risk life and limb to come to Europe? Some countries offer more in a life on the dole per month than the average GDP per capita back at home for some migrants. There is a clear incentive to move to Europe in spite of the high risk of injury or fatality. And given the demand of individuals who wish to establish themselves in Europe, there seems to be little concern about the future welfare of European nations; given that millions wish to migrate to Europe. What will happen to the house prices? Tax rates? Will public services, schools, and healthcare be overburdened? What about the national debts? There is a clear incentive structure to move to Europe in the here and now, but at what future cost? Will they kill the goose that lays the golden egg?

Push and Pull Incentive Factors:

Put bluntly, push factors are the whip and pull factors are a carrot dangling on a stick compelling individuals to drive forward striving towards the completion of a certain goal or satisfaction which they desire. Push is limitation, pull is temptation.

Push Factors

Structural and situational changes to one's choices partly out of one's control such as economics or family situation. Inflation, for example, reduces real wages and devalues money-savings pushing one to reevaluate their values and rearrange how they spend their money. Having a family changes one's values pushing them to prioritize their family. In prioritizing their family, the breadwinner(s) will look to work harder and longer hours, attain new qualifications, and ultimately, it is assumed, try to bring home the most bacon for their children to lavish them with the best possible upbringing. Push factors include limitations in one's decision-making, channeling the individual to make their final choice in shaping their personal value scales.

Pull Factors

Information compelling individual to wish to own a certain good or enjoy an experience. Information, in the form of advertisement or narratives spun by the Narrative Complex, create new desires which may never have occurred to the consumer. Technology which they may not have been aware of suddenly becomes the object of their desire. The facility in securing short term loans or using credit cards assists pull factors in adding to its tempting facade. Pull factors such as goods, new technologies, appealing thrills, appetizing food, etc, act as temptations to abandon a more future-oriented outlook in place of a more presentminded one.

CHAPTER 4

DEATH OF THE NUCLEAR FAMILY

THE DEATH OF THE NUCLEAR FAMILY has been nothing short of a tragic sickness ravaging western social life. The divorce rates speak for themselves. The best start you could give a child in life is two loving parents. Unfortunately, for many, this is just way too much to ask for. Single motherhood rates are soaring at a vast rate across various groups. Up until the introduction of the welfare state in the US (which I will address in my chapter on Economics), births outside of wedlock remained at a relatively stable rate of around 5% (2). The meteoric rise of births outside of wedlock—despite its absurd cheerleading from many talking heads and ivory tower feminists—indicates a drastic shifting of incentive structures; notwithstanding the wide availability of birth control(!).

Now, instead of tackling the issue head on, address-ing its financial and social costs, and attempting to minimize its spread; in many 'civilized' western social circles, it has been stigmatized to even dare question the unenviable plight of the individuals in question, who acted irresponsibly—something akin to congratulating and rewarding an alcoholic for falling off the wagon with a bottle of plonk. With the death of the nuclear family—or murder of the nuclear family—Western birthrates have fallen off a cliff, which is dreadful for the GDP Gods as less people means less immediate economic activity. Therefore, so-called 'replacement migration' (as put by the UN) has been employed to bridge the need for 3% growth by introducing new populations into society at an unprecedented rate. High time preference pursuits normalized in the 1960s replaced the low time preference pursuit of family life. High time preferences are, on the whole, selfishly motivated, and low time preferences on a social level facilitate cooperation. For a network of families to thrive, there needs to be mutually low time preferences and cooperation: something that has become lost over the past 2-3 generations.

It is evident that family life has become something unglamorous and a thing of the past, to some. There has been a weird promotion of all sorts of alternative, non-traditional family structures, while denigrating the previously normative arrangement—it simply ain't cool to want to bind yourself to the ol' ball n' chain. But now, we must approach the question at hand: what has this all got to do with time preferences? Well, having a family will rearrange most individual's perception of time. Instead of being a good consumer, attempting to fill the void in one's life with material possessions or experiences of little significance; their lives become invaluably enriched by the introduction of member(s) who will live beyond one's own life, and who will become—more often than not—one's priority. And this is how civilizations ripen: people working towards a common cause or purpose which they deem greater than themselves that will come to fruition and will be enjoyed long after they've perished. But we've seduced ourselves into believing utopian fantasies. Society is always in flux, there's no real utopian equilibrium to be reached. Society is something which must be preserved across generations. The family is the bedrock and spine to society. Everything else is secondary. The battered and tattered condition of the Western family, on the whole, is a sorry sight. Many have liberated themselves from the strictures of family life to fly off to experience hollow flings instead of a different, supposedly, more fulfilling, forms of gratification. A family gets in the way of cheap thrills. A family constricts your potentiality. The Narrative Complex told you that a family can be comprised of literally anybody. Hollywood shot movies and shows depicting family members as boring and stressful. Free yourself from their shackles of paralyzing ennui.

Without a family (or loved ones), there isn't much in place to make the person without a family think about the condition of the world after they've gone. This is one of the fundamental problems with many European political leaders without having any children of their own—Theresa May, Emmanuel Macron, Angela Merkel, Jean-Claude Juncker, et al—as they, ostensibly, have no skin in the game when they're out of office. Why would they care if their countries are wrecked if they won't be around to see it? And, besides, they can afford to live in a gated community and to employ bodyguards that the average Joe can't afford. The current political leaders who have promoted the policies which have most radically transformed their nations have been the ones who have nothing to preserve for their posterity. You'll have no skin in the game. Immediacy is of the essence. Tomorrow isn't as important as there are no dependents. There will be the realization of consequences to certain behaviors when children are added into the mix. Who wants responsibilities anyway? Children are an obstacle to present consumption as they are extra mouths to feed, siphoning funds away from your own ends. Being an empowered individual is a lot harder if you have a family. It isn't desirable. Don't become that boring square you rallied against in your teenage years. Kids will become your life, not you: which means that the world will cease to revolve around you.

Although women and mothers have always existed in the workforce in some way, the idyllic imagery of the 50's housewife and breadwinning husband is a little tough in the modern age on an average salary, despite GDP being far higher! Since the blistering eruption of the Civil Rights Era, women have become empowered to be high-flying career women to compete with men in the workforce. Sadly, even with assistance from anti-discrimination laws, this hasn't been the case. Not only is it unsustainable for many family to have one parent in the workforce, it has also become somewhat trendy for a mother to work, as well as doing one of the most demanding and important jobs in the world: mother-hood. In the name of equality, have many women become exhausted and overworked by juggling chil-dren, marriage, and career. Consequently, something has to give. That something can't be the kids—

obviously. It wouldn't be empowering to give up the career either; which only leaves a third. Coming home from work to find a messy home, needy kids and husband can't be something too appealing. In households where gender roles are more traditionally oriented, sexual intercourse is had, on average, on another 20 occasions a year compared to households which share chores. Households which share chores also tend to experience higher rates of fighting. Finally, if both parents are in the workforce, WHO raises the kids? It can't be the parents—they're working! The economic and social conditions which have drastically changed in the past few generations have created an incentive structure which promotes career, status, and money over the child. The press promotes stories on a regular basis discouraging having children for a multitude of inane reasons. Moreover, the difference in quality of raising a child between a mother and a random daycarer is rarely exposed in the press; giving modern families incomplete information in choosing how to raise their children, while both parents are off bringing home the bacon and being empowered. The willingness to choose material pursuits instead of the child's wellbeing—whether by necessity or vanity—indicates a higher time preference due to an incompleteness of the information at hand since there is no substituting a parent at home for a stressed-out daycarer looking after several other children who aren't their own. There are, indeed, potentially long lasting emotional consequences felt by the child in their daily abandonment to a daycarer. These consequences aren't directly felt by the parent, but transferred onto the child as the parent pursues other ends.

Children need their parents. Both of them. Often-times, not deferring the social gratification of feeling/looking empowered means that the children will foot the bill. And former children are currently footing the bill for the high time preferences of previous generations. Instead of taking responsibility in the present, succeeding generations have shouldered the burdens laid upon them for the immediate gratification of others. Now, in America, there's a national debt spiraling out of control; unfunded liabilities costing in the hundreds of trillions; and, most crucially: an unsustainable Ponzi Scheme state pension which has been foisted upon the current generation, set up in lieu of the children the preceding generations didn't have. Along with the unassailable levels of debt dumped on the younger generations, came the sexual liberation movement, birth control, then abortions (as if birth control wasn't enough); seemingly because many were incapable of deferring gratification. Plus, if you can't get laid through your looks and charms, or afford a sex worker, you can always rub one out over your favorite porn site. Heck, porn is cool nowadays, there are no consequences for becoming psychologically dependent on pleasuring yourself over self-abasing actors living emotionally unhealthy lives, performing unrealistic acts. I mean, how dare you think womyn have no agency?! You must be some form of incel loser to be against women emotionally and physically harming themselves in this lucrative occupation—so just fap away, sweaty (sweetie); who hurt you, boo? For guys—and girls—who may not be as sexually attractive or have low self-esteem/social confidence, pornography is an easily accessible means to *ahem* relieve oneself. Unfortunately, instead of deferring gratification, working on becoming more sexually attractive and/or confident; opening up your browser takes less time and scratches that itch far quicker, radically changing the former incentive structure where courtship or wooing somebody which takes time would have to take place before bedding that person. Even with a plethora of products and methods to prevent pre-marital or undesired conception, there's still a need for abortion, indicating either a lack of care or immaturity when dealing with one's reproductive health, given how rampant abortion has become. Recently, in New York, abortions after twenty-one weeks were three times higher than the 2015 homicide rate. Being responsive solely to one's impulses have enduring social conse-quences.

One of the most commonly cited reasons given for divorce is financial issues. Financial problems can be remedied with time. However, impatience can creep in and act as a more powerful motivator than the potential for a brighter future which has yet to materialize. We don't even have patience for our children. With the rise of the term "Daycare Generation" where more career-minded couples/mothers, less-financially able couples/ mothers, or simply uncaring families abandon their children to be raised by others. The Daycare Generation receive values and discipline outside of the scope of their families. Children need their parents. A Daycarer is in no way fit to replace the parent, unless the parent is abusive to the child. The Daycarer is usually stressed out by the other crying toddlers under their temporary guardianship and cannot pay equal attention to them all. The Daycarer also won't radiate the same love and affection towards the child as a biological parent. No amount of trendy pseudophilosophizing or modern studies, in earnest, state convincingly otherwise. Leaving the child in Daycare does a tremendous disservice to the upbringing of the child, potentially risking their emotional health. And what attitudes towards parenting will be adopted by the child raised by the Daycarer, provided they actually have children of their own? It seems as if the apple don't fall too far from the tree. Child abuse is seemingly passed on intergenerationally in various case—will a dearth in caring for one's children be passed on too? The possibility of Daycare offers an individual the ability to temporarily transfer the responsibility of parenting while they pursue selfish ends. The consequence of this probably won't eat away at the conscience of the parent, but to be felt by the child and their children. The inability to take responsibility for one's actions comes from the transferral of consequence. There aren't any real forms of social disapproval, as consequence, to temporarily abandoning one's children for one trendy reason or another. The fact remains, a Daycarer can never love a child as much as a parent. A child will be receptive to their deficiency in receiving love. How will their ability to love their children, spouse, and friends be affected?

Immediately after the sexual liberation came an inexorable shift in consciousness away from the intended purposes of marriage: sex. Of course, without proceeding naively, fornication always occurred; but never to the level of—not just acceptance—but of rabid tolerance that we ubiquitously witness today. Being able to control one's impulses and to defer gratification is something that separates humans from animals. Not succumbing to every urge IS an almost exclusively human endeavor, as we can rationalize the possibility of negative avoidable consequences that may arise from succumbing to our impulses. Although sexual liberation has been associated with notions of 'progress', we've only progressed towards the animal kingdom in the process. People who wished to withhold sex until marriage or meeting somebody worthwhile, in some circles, are mocked as prudes, equated to practicing something debunked and archaic. The rise in contraception, the "Morning After" pill, and abortion has created an incentive structure where the consequences for one's actions in not deferring gratification have been practically removed. Moreover, if you happen to get pregnant, not to worry, you can always claim a check from the government or child support from the father. Children of divorced parents tend to have less satisfaction from their relationships and a higher likelihood to end in divorce, forming a vicious cycle of divorce, broken homes, and an incomplete upbringing for their children. At least the Narrative Complex will offer them solace, convince them of the empowerment of their decisions, assure them that their children won't just be raised adequately, but better! Friends spiritually invested in the same Narrative Complex' narrative will also offer formidable support and comfort, parroting the same churned out production-line cliches. The need for reassurance under the guise of empowering individualism is a disguise for a lack of self-respect so profound that it reverberates onto their children, increasing the likelihood to diminish their confidence in their future relationships. With exceptions such as abuse, many reasons to break a family apart are in the parent's immediate self-interests—high time preferences. Instead of sticking by somebody who may not be the best partner, the baby is thrown out with the bath water. Suggesting that restraint can be practiced in a position where the sexually active consenting parties is treated as a snide method of undermining a woman's empowerment to choose the sex she wishes to partake in. There is every form of contraception—and heck, even pulling out—to avoid the conception of an unwanted child, yet abortion is still an option. All the financial consequences of sex, where the consenting parties aren't in a stable or loving position to raise a child, have been removed for the woman, at least. This means that the need to overcome urges which the overwhelmingly vast majority of people experience—to have sex—have been eliminated, reducing us to a more primitive and decivilized approach in who we choose to copulate with. Time preferences, in this respect, can be afforded to be high. The immediate incentive is that sex is wonderful, pleasurable, socially acceptable, and a deep emotional commitment doesn't have to be made, with most negative consequences eliminated.

Contemporary liberal forms of parenting do a general disservice to the child. In extremely progressive milieux it is all the rage to raise a child gender neutral, until the child develops something of a conscience and determines their own gender, despite the fact that observable gender roles develop from a young age when children are handed certain toys. This is a more extreme example of the willy-nilly, live-and-let-live form of "parenting" practiced in the supposedly more socially advanced cities of the west. Giving the child slack or being lax when it comes to punishment (don't get me wrong, I AM NOT ADVOCATING FOR CORPORAL PUNISHMENT) may be detrimental to their moral ormation in later life. Of course, it requires discipline, time, and repetition to instill good/desirable behaviors into a child. Being overly permissive, or, in many cases, not tending to the child at all and throwing a tablet or a phone to distract the child so that mommy can watch her soap can be ruinous to the child's upbringing. Raising a child without discipline is akin to growing an unsecured vine: the vine will grow all over the place, creep and contort itself into impossible tangles, wander into openings, wrap itself around things it shouldn't, and its fruit won't be as impressive. A low parental investment strategy (r-selection) becomes more useful in a chaotic environment. Here, our current environment, at least when it comes to truth, is wholly chaotic. Information constantly changes and the almost universal availability of social media enables almost everyone to become privy to those constant changes. Much of the chaos has come about from a general shift towards high time preferences, the social acceptance of high time preferences, and the Narrative Complex innumerable narratives and metanarratives. Out of a more laissez-faire approach to sexuality, comes a more laissez-faire approach to childrearing. Children are impressionable. If hypersexuality becomes normative, the children will follow. Widespread hypersexuality can only exist where high time preferences are the norm and incentive structures have been adjusted via social acceptance and Narrative Complex propaganda to complement such a hypersexualization.

Not only has marriage become desacralized by the cheapening of sex, but also, those who are most generous in engaging in sexual intercourse tend to shun sex for its real purpose: procreation. I have already mentioned the rise in preventative measures which can be taken to have "safe" sex, such as contraceptives, the "morning after" pill, and abortions; but there seems to be a new trend where young adults deliberately—and permanently—remove themselves from the genepool by some form of irreversible medical treatment. Children only get in the way, right? There have been many reasons for why people claim to not want to have children, ranging from: "they get in the way", "I want to focus on my career", "I'm white and white people shouldn't breed", "I can't do X, Y, or Z if I have kids", etc. No matter what excuse is offered, there seem to be two underlying themes to each excuse: self-hatred and narcissism. Individuals who are so averse to having children are often known as Anti-Natalists. Not wishing to have children because they made intrude on one's oh-so-fulfilling life, in order for them to "do what they want" and not having to defer gratification, comes across only as a, veiled, prolonged form of suicide. It is a prolonged form of suicide as the genes end with that individual, their perception of time ends with them, and what would be their impact after they've gone if they were to decide to take their lives sooner? Anti-natalism is one of the highest expressions of nihilism as life in itself is so valueless that it isn't worth passing on one's genes. Refusing to have children without the trade off for a higher purpose is unnatural at best. So what needs to be done—other than filling one's life with as many pleasure-inducing experiences as possible, if everything begins and ends with you?

One of the best things one can do to avoid poverty, statistically speaking, is to get married. However, avoiding poverty isn't enough to incentivize marriage. Movements such as MGTOW (Men Go Their Own Way) have arisen as a reaction to modern feminism and other prevailing socially-accepted political sub-movements and trends which supposedly empower women and magnify their pre-existing hypergamy. Men who belong to such movements whose mission is to avoid the modern woman fear risking their finances, resources, reputation, home, car, everything by betting on the wrong horse, or, in this case, bride. What's in it for them? Their perception of the modern woman is a viperous parasite like the spawn from the movie Alien—sucking on the victim's face only to have its offspring burst through the victim's chest, breaking the victim's heart. The risk outweighs the reward. Divorce courts are highly skewed to the woman's favor in child custody, damages, awards, etc. In many cases of spousal abuse—

even if it is the man who is on the receiving end of the abuse—the police will arrest the man. These men would rather turn away from marriage entirely, seeing it as a form of the game, 'Minesweeper'. As an alarming amount of marriages end in divorce, indicating both a loss of faith in religion underpinning the importance of marriage and high time preferences in ending the relationship instead of reconciling their differences. Abstaining from marriage isn't replaced by long term fulfillment. Substitutes for marriage involve vanishing dopamine hits in the form of vapid entertainment instead of something sustainable. For women, there's always the risk of choosing a partner who's a deadbeat, a drunk, a playa, or abusive. However, marriage is still one of the most effective methods for women to astronomically increase their wealth. Assuming the end goal for marriage is children, children should be enough of an incentive in itself. But it is not enough. There is a lack of care. Sometimes individuals dive in head first to a marriage without properly assessing their future spouse, leading to disaster. Liberation from responsibility and consequence is an integral part in modern incentive structures—but this is nothing but a poorly dressed form of selfishness stemming from a needlessness for duty or sacrifice as a result of the obsolescence of higher purposes, transcendental values, or something greater than oneself.

Death of the Nation

The nation is a group of, on the whole, genetically

similar tribes/communities/settlements with a shared language, history, culture, mythology, faith, and state/political union. Whether a nation practises more decentralized forms of politics is, here, irrelevant. In the modern age, the term "nation" has gained negative connotations given the West's bloody history and the term "nationalist" has become something of a pejorative, often followed by "far-right", "ultra-right", or "Neo-Nazi" when used by the mainstream media. National-ism has earned itself a reprehensible reputation for the actions of a few self-seeking, corrupt, and incompetent statesmen scheming to improve their own personal standing which has meaninglessly cost the lives of tens of millions in the last century alone. As a result, the baby has been thrown out with the bath water. Nationalism is a dirty word. In our expanding globalist economy where talent is scouted from everywhere, yesterday's xeno-phobia is an unwelcome guest within the Kumbaya neoliberal tapestry woven by our intellectual superiors.

Our intellectual superiors are, although, shielded from the consequences of their actions. It is the working and lower-middle classes who are receive the full brunt of the neoliberal policies. Industry flees; communities left destitute; state dependency runs riot; drug and alcohol abuse rise. Suicide and drug overdoses, in many industrially abandoned areas, have begun to outpace deaths by car accidents. We have tricked ourselves into believing that economic productivity is akin to quality of life, when it couldn't be further from the truth. And while millions, which, in order to escape their country's crippling poverty and lack of opportunity; full integration often means becoming absorbed into a cultureless goop which has been fallaciously implied to resemble so-called "Western values". Western values, over the past 4-5 generations, has become a deeply embellished term whose meaning can be repurposed in order to shoehorn specific policies often deleterious to Western interests. There is no expectation for newly arrived groups to integrate into their host nations. Suggestions prompting individuals to assimilate into their new countries will be often met with a barrage of invective volleyed at the racist who so dared to make the initial suggestion. In fact, native Westerners are the one's who are behooved to integrate into their fast-changing societies. If they don't, they're the ones in the wrong. Consequently, we witness a situation where Westerners are urged to renounce their consciousness as part as an individual nation—flags are torn down, their histories denigrated, their heroes vilified, their myths debunked, their public holidays deemed racist—but new arrivals are fully encouraged to celebrate their cultures. Naysayers are scolded. Are we to expect unity or balkanization? What are the incentives to integration, if integration is discouraged?

As I have mentioned, the nation, on the the whole, is built up of genetically similar individuals. The nation could be perceived as an agglomeration of tribes seeking to defend their own interests. The tribe is an extension of the family. Despite much universalist propaganda spewed by the intelligentsia over decades: most people will never care for a stranger—irrespective of nationality—as much as their own kin. Most people will favor their own compatriots over a foreigner, as they will love their family over another's; as they'll cherish their history over another's.

For this, I made be called a zealous bigot by some; or, alternatively, those who'd prefer to associate with their own countryfolk—probably the vast majority of the world's population—may be called xenophobes, but only if they're white. And for this, it must be understood that Western histories were always multicultural: Londinium was a sprawling cosmopolitan paradise, the Nordic Bronze Age was hella diverse, and other questionable revisionist hot takes which have been promoted by globalist outlets by design—to deracinate Western identities by severing ties to their histories and to encourage mass immigration under the pretense of reauthenticating Western history as previously multicultural. The most fanatical globalists who aren't part of the Narrative Complex don't despise their nation's history by accident, but by design. By mutilating their bond to their history, they long for nothing to preserve, but to destroy—yet there is no real blueprint for a superior society to be constructed out the rubble of the West. The force is destruction. It's entropy. It's decay. It won't enlighten or improve. To want to preserve something, there must be a certain connection to the past. The future must come as second nature, so that we wish to defer gratification far into it—after our time is up. Those who aren't connected to the past through intense reeducation via the Narrative Complex enthusiastically warning them of the evils of their forebears—slavery, genocide, colonialism, etc—seem lost, in desperate need to construct new and inauthentic sub-identities to fit in, playing off modern gender theory and claiming to identify with genders outside of the male-female spectrum or to identify as being animals. Many of these individuals often exploit a mental illness they may be suffering as part of their identity. Why should they be made to suffer for things they didn't do? Mongolians couldn't care less about the rape, murder, genocide, and pillaging of Genghis Khan; in fact, they honor his historical image with statues. But Americans are guilted into dismantling statues of second-rate commanders of a civil war which literally decimated their population. Guilt, deconstruction, and vilification for the actions of our ancestors is largely what inculcates a recurring theme of hopelessness, tarting up the idea of consumption as a diversion away from the looming sense of hopelessness materialized by constant attacks from the Narrative Complex.

Nationalism is a permanent source of political energy that can be extracted and harnessed by statesmen—both honorable and dishonorable—making it a potent political double-edged sword. When the nation is under threat, palpable levels of energy reverberate throughout the land, awakening a sense of solidarity only seen in crises. Many individuals who lived through great wars often report these wartorn periods as being the happiest times of their lives; not for living under constant threat, but because their existence has been given a higher meaning and an unseen level of trust, building, community, togetherness, solidarity, and purpose is felt. All other ends are substituted for one higher common goal—which has been lost as a result of the awesome growth in material wealth, comfort, and ubiquitous modern philosophies whose very existence is at odds with past values such as the nation state. This particular paragraph may be sit as well as eating an oyster left on the counter on a hot day, but, if we are to be honest, it's mere human nature to care and love one's own family above a stranger's. We would be incapable of surviving without such a strategy. One of the many reasons why the nuclear family is so relentlessly criticized, satirized, and demonized by the Narrative Complex is that it is a bulwark to the expansion of the State and to the formation of a one-world government. The fabric of the nation must be entirely denatured in order for individuals to acquiesce to the formation of a supranational, one-size-fits-all gubernamental superstructure. Cultures need to be diluted for power to be centralized in order to, a priori, prevent a willingness for communities to breakaway. And it all begins with the family. A strong family unit's priorities and value scales are more in line with longer term gratification instead of immediate gratification. Having a family should imply low time preferences. To kill the nation, the family must go. Some may say that family structures must evolve according to the times. Others may argue that the family is outdated and prevents wamen from unlocking their potentiality. In reality, those bitterly opposed to the family are almost always opposed to the nation, as the nation is the extension of the family. A cultureless goop isn't a nation, but a country—or even a geographic economic region with a healthy GDP! Who would want to defer gratification beyond their own life if this is their future: no nation, no family; but Brutalism, heterogeny, consumerism, and self-loathing?

Private enterprise—capitalism—has brought unprecedented material wealth to millions and has lifted billions out of poverty. Nevertheless, private enterprise has brought unprecedented challenges. The abundant wealth created by private enterprise has brought people, who, under no other previous historical circumstances, would come into contact with one another. Now, people have been endowed with the ability to up sticks and relocate to wherever in the world they'd like, on a whim. Neat, huh? The main drawback is that people don't feel as much of an attachment to their homelands as in the past; and are, therefore. less likely to wish for the longevity of their nation without such an attachment. In America, for example, tens of millions of Central Americans have moved up north and have clustered around the South West where they elect representatives of from their own in-groups—naturally. In Yorkshire, UK, where thousands of Pakistanis have been relocated, politicians of Pakistani descent have been elected— naturally. If these individuals were fully integrated, then why is there the need to vote in people who share their culture, history, and language? Why are they so racist? Why haven't they adopted the individualistic tenets pertinent to Anglospheric values? LOL. But it is only natural for individuals to act in an unfamiliar environment. Given the fact that their are millions who love and would give up their lives for their new host nations; the current trend appears to be the opposite. Western history has been mercilessly revised and mistated by much of the professoriate class to push a subversive political agenda and to aggravate minority groups into taking more radical approaches to political action, while weakening any potential reactionaries by making their past and their platforms indefensible. Minorities are led to feel as if they've been historically wronged by their host nation. The only cure for these historical wrongdoings amplified by the chatterati is to transfer more power and resources to hostile minority groups while they lead the cheer to the West's downfall.

We also live in the age of transnational treaties, unions, and supragovernmental organizations starting with the so-called "Progressive Era" beginning at the Spanish-American War peaking with Woodrow Wilson's involvement in The First World War in the name of "self-determination" and making the World "safe for Democracy". While there had been previous international alliances, the first alliance to begin a global hegemony promoting the globalist ideological values that have evolved into modern neoliberalism was The League Of Nations. Since the two World Wars, there has been a rise in the transnational agreements, treaties, unions, etc, culminating in the EU, NAFTA, TPP, Mercosur, etc, which have been formed under the banner of "free trade", but sneakily increase a centralization of power and an adjoining reduction in national sovereignty. There's nothing free about it!

Many of these transnationals, whose bureaucrats are unelected, override the laws of member states. Historically, vassalage hasn't been very popular. The most ardent supporters of these transational groups are usually overeducated middle class individuals who have been spoon-fed the Narrative Complex' narratives from an early age, lullabied into believing the soporific globalist tune of the intelligentsia. A lot of individuals living within these supranational political unions express their discontent by electing politicians, unscripted to the narrative, who promise to put their nations first, into power—much to the discontent of enthusiasts of these transnational organizations. Corporations and states alike have formed an ungodly marriage to undermine the welfare of the nation in favor of short-term gain. Supragovernmental transnational organizations have formed so-called "free trade" zones where borders have been forcibly wedged open for the nimble transfer of capital and labor to where large multinational enterprises can reap in whopping profits at the expense of disenfranchised and deindustrialized nations. These transnational supragovermnetal organizations have latched onto so-called "free trade" and multinationals have latched onto these supragovernmental organizations in a bizarre form of mutual parasitism where neither parasite can afford to kill their munificent hosts. Neither of them could exist without each other, rendering them utterly co-dependent. But, let's be frank, the most-cited reason why nationalism is surging is because of mass immigration. The neoliberal left needs votes, the neoliberal right needs cheap labor; and, as part of the physical nature of the state, it needs an excuse to expand. In order to claim viability into the future, clearly defined cultures need to be diluted and restated to concede room to this elitist ideology. It's the current year! Without the bureaucratic monstrosity headquartered in Brussels, who knows… maybe Europe would've erupted into another war had it not been for the divine wisdom of the neoliberal plutocrats—which is why extinguishing European candour is necessary. If it weren't for the EU, the availability of certain products would plummet; seeing consumer goods become more expensive—you wouldn't want that, would you? Off the back of this neo-Babylonian experiment, there seems to be a general despair among many of its unofficial supporters. High time preferences seem to dictate its support. Cheap consumer goods, the ability to travel across borders unimpeded, nice holidays, and fleeting experiences are what attract many supporters of globalist causes. Faith in the nation has been lost as a result of tireless anti-Western propagandizing. Hatred of one's own group or causes linked to protecting the environment are employed as reasons to avoid having children. Both men and women alike, at the height of their fertilities, have taken to social media to boast of their irreversible tube snipping/tying procedures, rendering them incapable of having children so that they can freely enjoy a life of impulse and debauchery. If who they are, their nations, and achievements weren't so ruthlessly undermined on a daily basis; maybe they wouldn't have plunged in headfirst, relegating themselves to an empty life of shortlasting, vanishing thrills.

I have previously stated that the term nationalist is something of a pejorative. The intelligentsia (media, academia, etc) has browbeaten the average Joe into negatively associating—something like a Pavlovian response—their nation, thereby demoralizing them, and shepherding them into acquiescing to mass migration and the formation of supranational organizations. According to Spectator Index, here is who would fight for their nation:

Morocco: 94%

Pakistan: 89%

Vietnam: 89%

India: 75%

Turkey: 73%

China: 71%

Indonesia: 70%

Israel: 66%

Russia: 59%

Nigeria: 50%

Brazil: 48%

US: 44%

Canada: 30%

Australia: 29%

France: 29%

UK: 27%

Italy: 20%

Germany: 18%

Japan: 11%

Refusing to fight for one's nation indicates a lack of care in the result of its future. A prevailing immediacy of thought and selfishness—a dereliction of what was formerly duty. Detachment to one's nation furthers the hampering lack of identity shouldered by many. There's no point to lower your time preferences for a contemptible nation. There's no point in stolidly taking the slings and arrows in defending your nation's interests. Most people buckle at the prospect of being irremediably painted as a racist. The undertowing immediate gratification in avoiding the six-letter is too strong. If you wouldn't even make the ultimate sacrifice in defending your country, what are the odd's you'd risk getting called racist for pointing out the unsustainability of mass immigration?

Not many people would make the ultimate sacrifice for a multicultural economic zone where GDP trumps social cohesion and happiness. Why would you give your life to a country that did bad things several generations ago? Why have children who will continue the legacy of such an evil fabric? It's time to end it here. Share your land and resources with millions who don't share your history, language, or faith, and who harbor nothing but contempt for your existence. This is the way forward. This is progress. Your moral and intellectual superiors in the Narrative Complex all endorse this. You'll get a well-deserved dopamine hit in uncritically agreeing with them. Now, you're an intellectual, too. You deserve your smug wry smile. Don't you dare let cognitive dissonance slide his malodorous foot through the door. Just go with the pontificating intellectuals; this is their life. They know better. Social trust is nothing but a social construct. However, without social trust there cannot exist the cooperation and conditions necessary to foster low time preferences. People will wall themselves off from society and live more for today, as the future looks dim.

With family life becoming more and more unfeasible, the nation being a concept that only seduces racists, and God for sky-daddy worshiping dimwits, nobody has anything to die for anymore. Some would call this liberating: as now, people won't aimlessly lose their lives over outdated superstitions/constructs; I am more of the opinion that without having anything greater than oneself to die for, the individual has nothing to live for. That is not, to say, to go kamikaze on the minutest threat to one's family. But the unwillingness to giving oneself to a greater cause indicates a form of both cowardice and narcissism—a narcissism fully endorsed by the prevailing consumerist pseudo-philosophy that passes as progress. One could look askance at such an idea. Looking at oneself as the epitome of being limits oneself to oneself, equalling spiritual poverty. The nation, qua extension of the family, is assumed to live on beyond one's own life or at least is expected to. Many men in the first half of the twentieth century laid down their lives before sowing their oats in the presumed knowledge their lives weren't sacrificed in vain. Their perceived time would far exceed the perceived time of today which has been abruptly shortened by the prevailing consumerist pseudo-philosophy which has tumescently grown out of the whimpering demise of the nation state directly after the end of the Second World War.

Without the concept of a nation—in fact, with the

concept of the nation being something execrable—time preferences of anti-nationalists or globalists will be higher (present-minded) as there is no territory drawn up by supposedly invisible lines to preserve for posterity. Anti-natalism or childlessness and cosmopolitanism seem to go hand-in-hand. To the cosmopolitan, the nation is an obstacle to their fleeting personal ends— vanishing dopamine hits. By not having a nation or even a regional community to preserve and cherish, the individual's interests may flip to become more present-minded or vapid. Local communities have been delivered a fatal blow by globalism. The choice is clear: face state-dependency, destitution, and addiction, or, learn to code and immerse yourself as part of an expanding, diverse, global community. Don't like it? Well, tough. You'll be fired, your name sullied, and become unmarriable. The incentive structure makes your grandfather's way of life untenable. You are to be deterritorialized and thrown into an unwelcoming, unhuman environment. If you're not desiring production, you can't be a cog in the technocapitalist machine. Ostracism is a powerful conditioning tool. In human history, society has never progressed (I say 'progress' neutrally) so quickly. Values, information, choices, and incentive structures have never moved at such a fast pace. When information shifts so rapidly, how can one have low time preferences if their current information becomes obsolete before the time they wish to receive gratification? A tree simply cannot live if it is uprooted and replanted every week. "Living for today" is the only possible mantra when everything changes tomorrow. In order to stay ahead of the curve, the proverbial drawing board has to be revisited on a regular basis. And being a good consuming-producer enables you to play a part in the modern world. You wouldn't want to be left behind, now, would you?

Since the end of the Second World War and the end of Western Colonialism, mass immigration from former colonies and other nations has ramped up in intensity over the past six decades, accelerating in the mid-90s in the UK, and reaching warp speed in Northern Europe 2015 with the so-called "Migrant Crisis". America's immigration policy gradually changed since the 19th century, culminating in the 1965 Immigration Act, which shifted America's predominantly Eurocentric immigration to one which prioritized the Third World—en masse. Harvard professor, Robert Putnam, conducted a controversial study that defied his preconceptions on multiculturalism which led him to suppress the diffusion of his study for years. He found that: in more multicultural communities, social trust is lowered and people tend to become more introverted. A more introverted society which isn't so centered around the community is less likely to invest time or to have a lower time preference for their neighbors. The possibility for great social capital declines as socializing as a pastime, rather than introversion, also declines. Consequently, the state or even certain private businesses may have to intervene as mediators or services providers where social distrust runs high, for example: in child minding for the daycare generation, more policing to smooth over social conflicts, more schooling and extra teaching staff, polyglot services, translations, etc. In more homogeneous societies, more social capital is produced through voluntary association, springing from closer familial proximity. Investing in one's community, provided that social trust remains high, often pays dividends throughout one's life. Furthermore, lower time preferences with one's immediate community cultivates solidarity. Higher time preferences sows distrust as, as atomized individuals, the benefits reaped from acting untoward or dishonestly may exceed the benefits from investing time or forming lasting relationships with the community. Instead—in both big cities and rural settlements—we've seen a jump in alienation and atomization. In cities, we've seen a dip in cohesion and a spike in crime. In the American countryside, there's an appalling opioid crisis ravaging Rustbelt towns and villages where these drugs aren't solely used to dull physical pain, but, also, a spiritual pain manifesting as hopelessness. It takes low time preferences to forge lasting social trust. Bonds take time to form. If one were simply living for today, their relationships with their peers would be redrawn to cater for their high time preferences, and friendships would be more superficial. The gratification from being part of a high-trust society—where impulses are caged to avoid jeopardizing the community's integrity, for example, avoiding adultery, theft, physical violence, etc—comes more in the form of dripfed dividends rather than a windfall. The peace of mind and reliance that comes as a result is far greater than any immediate gratification which may arise from breaching said trust. Furthermore, one's children can inherit a strong social bond in such a high-trust society. But that society's demographics must remain relatively stable and homogeneous to avoid endangering its integrity. Values, information, language, religion, etc, must be aligned to ensure its lasting integrity and for divisions to be avoided. Stability is a necessary precondition to having low time preferences because the amount of possible social risks between the present and future gratification are minimized, as opposed to a more chaotic social order.

Fear of being called "racist" in defending the interests of a nation against rapid change is a question of high time preferences. Valuing the avoidance of being called racist by somebody subscribed to the prevailing socially-accepted politics other attempting to avert an imminent danger which may present itself as a more unpleasant experience than being called racist. Choosing the path of least resistance signifies instant gratification in wanting to be left alone or not having to deal with the consequences of a witchhunt accusing one of being racist. Those who realize their countries are in decline, but would avoid the six-letter smear act selfishly, particularly if they have children. It also indicates a loss of vigor and energy behind their beliefs. Fear of a six-letter word is a little too much to handle and the reward for avoiding it is, seemingly, too great in the short term.

All in all, the death of the nation makes for a more presentminded society. By relinquishing a nation to preserve for one's people and a unique way of life, an incentive structure is in place which disincentivises having low time preferences. There has been another untimely death: the death of eternity, as a concept. Very few wish to see their nations die, but, as I'm gloomily suggested, the (Western) nation will become a little more than a multicultural economic zone, lazily clinging onto superficial traditions—as long as they don't interfere with globalization or antagonize one of the many diverse groups who happen to reside within that nation. Leaving something behind for a nation which doesn't resemble the one built by their ancestors won't become as desirable. So, what will happen instead? In a word: consumption—consumption of resources; consumption of savings; consumption of energy; consumption of spirit; consumption of soul. Until there's nothing left.

CHAPTER 5

MEDIA, ENTERTAINMENT, AND INFORMATION

THE MAINSTREAM MEDIA DOESN'T EXIST TO INFORM: it exists to paint a narrative, construct a reality for the public which protects the interests of the establishment—and then change that reality by spinning, then floating, new narratives/information to never let the dust settle, creating a tactical form of chaos to give themselves validity. Nothing we know is allowed to be everlasting. Everything has to be subjective, except the intrinsic evil of those who dwell outside the orbit of prevailing socially-accepted politics. And this fabricated hyper-subjectivity is by design. With no identifiable values, values are easily constructed to suit and cement the status of the powers that be. Time preferences are bound to be high if our knowledge and values are constantly evolving at a fast pace. How do you keep time prefer-ences low if information and values are, a priori, unrecognizable in the not-so-distant future or if every-thing is relative? Even language evolves at a sprint. Acceptable politically correct language changes before our very eyes. How can something mainstream a few years ago cause offence today? The people who claim offence only do so because they know it commands them power in the present. No long distance planning or hard work is required to command power from claiming offence as it's capricious. Who decides what is and isn't—factually and morally? Our morally superior chattering classes are comprised of the brightest and best who've been through the approved channels: public/private education (little difference in curricula), Ivy League/top colleges, living in ideologically identical social bubbles in big cities, etc. Differing in opinion results in social suicide. In a world where lasting relations are becoming increasingly difficult to form and often require time, time with which people are very miserly; it's often easier to go with the flow and to accept the prevailing consensus. The establishment, from an early age, can corrale the sharpest tools in the shed to continue disseminating information which protects the interests of both the establishment and the intelligentsia. What would happen if, for instance, a reputable establishment thinker such as Paul Krugman were to suddenly turn 180 and go against the narrative? It would spell social suicide, his name sullied, his book sales plummeting through the floor, the loss of his NYT column, etc. Even establishment lapdogs have a clear incentive structure. Very few will willingly answer to their morals and reject the wealth, fame, power, and influence they wield. And on the question of time preferences, although many in positions of power may flirt with reputation-damaging scandals, most of which are a testament to their low-impulse control; there simply any major consequences to their actions as long as their views match those of the prevailing socially-accepted politics. The media will apologetically absolve them of their indiscretions. The children and families of those in the establishment are protected by the establishment. Their scions are practically set for life if they toe the party line. And why wouldn't they? The fact is, as long as they unwaveringly support the prevailing socially-accepted politics, there are no consequences to any dirty, underhanded, or degenerate shenanigans they get up to. They are society's moral progenitors and enforcers. They are above the law. You're the pariah who must genuflect for their magnanimity and forgiveness.

Those in charge of the media, as I've previously stated, exists only to paint a narrative. This is because everything is political. Nothing is safe from politics. Nothing can avoid its grasp for long. And everything will be injected by its venom. Everything outside your family that you love is tainted by politics. Woke capital is real. The Civil Rights era protestors now occupy the board rooms of vast multinationals. Corporations can project their politics as part of their mission statement or via social media to garner support. Stocks can take a hit if it means that companies can virtue signal about the latest political trend. Even though the stereotypical sports fan is a high testosterone jock male of limited intelligence sports companies and clubs can alienate their core demographic by ramming unsolicited political vistas down the throats of disgruntled fans. It won't matter, the long term consequences, in a lot of instances, will be negligible. In the here and now, viewing figures may take a tumble. But this is worthwhile in the long term as a socially alienated demographic will marinate in the prevailing socially-accepted politics long enough for it to percolate into their consciousness, thus becoming acceptable in the future. This is a method by which the establishment can sow seeds demoralizing a change-resistant demographic, thus desensitizing them to prevailing socially-accepted politics and making them more presentminded.

The truth in itself doesn't matter. What matters is that the truth of the prevailing socially-accepted political narrative is accepted as truth. If the media says it, it must be so. If Hollywood represents current social dynamics, it is how it is. If your Humanities professor tells you that whiteness is inherently evil, then, it must be so. Unfortunately, what they say or portray might not coincide with reality. You feel a tugging sensation inside. You begin to squint or scrunch your face when you read the odd editorial. That latest movie you saw had a very forced script; the characters didn't represent any scenarios you're familiar with. Your professor said something which was the opposite of your personal experience. The tugging sensation gets unbearable. The trust you had confided in these outlets begins to falter. You do your own research and come to the realization that disapproved outlets and books paint a picture closer to your experiences and observations in the world. Congratulations, you've taken your first red pill. That tugging sensation was your conscience; that feeling is known as 'cognitive dissonance'. In spite of the correlation between low time preferences and intelligence; being invested in the Narrative Complex' representation of reality—or narrative—shifts focus away from an intelligent usage of time geared towards the future, to a focus that is more presentminded in nature, because of the selective nature of the information given to the public.

There are many real world observations which are misaligned to the prevailing narrative. Take, for example, hate crimes. Many alleged hate crimes are reported, blown out of proportion by the mainstream media, then quietly forgotten once they've been disproven. I think everyone who's ever tuned into CNN will know more about President Trump's unusual dietary habits than their own in-laws'. The media commands everyone how to feel and not to think. You are to feel a certain way about X, Y, or Z event, not to critically analyse it—that's the job for your favorite approved newspaper's Sunday columnist. Moreover, you will be grotesquely maligned for deviating off the narrative. I've taken the liberty to add the following problem/answers:

- Against mass immigration? You're far-right.
- Against islamization of western cities? You're islamophobic.
- For traditional marriage? You're homophobic.
- For Trump/Brexit? You're uneducated/racist/backwards/white

And you probably read the Daily Mail, to cap it off. And if you read or believe anything from the naughty publications, you must be an idiot. A recent meme sparked tremendous controversy after several users were banned from social media for posting it. This was known as the 'NPC meme'. NPC is a gaming reference to nonplayer character which is pre-programmed to have set language and actions which the gamer cannot control. The NPC in real life is somebody who robotically regurgitates the same vacuous epithets when confronted by information or arguments which contradict the prevailing socially-accepted politics. This meme struck a nerve, since social media sites felt it necessary to suspend users. Some of the memes portrayed NPCs incapable of entertaining opposing ideas and simply shortcircuiting then resorting to hurling insults and buzzwords. What the NPC meme depicts is a cult-follower; somebody married to the prevailing socially-accepted politics. The cognitive dissonance felt by the depictions in the memes demonstrates a pitiful level of emotional maturity. But, there's a lot on the line to genuinely entertain views that emanate from the stinkin' mouths of the most morally repugnant individuals: racists. Only mouthbreathing racists could possibly read the Daily Mail. The Narrative Complex has made cognitive dissonance commonplace: if one was to insult the intelligence of somebody they deemed racist—anybody who doesn't subscribe to prevailing socially-accepted politics is racist—they'd be egged on by their prevailing socially-accepted politics peers; but, if somebody were to suggest that a certain group had less performative intelligence than another, that's racist and unacceptable. To the Narrative Complex, freethinking rational individuals would be useless to their incentive structure. Those who questioned the legitimacy of their views are problematic. The Narrative Complex needs individuals almost wholly dependent on their emotional faculties to continue to consume their truth. The prevailing socially-accepted politics has drawn millions to its narrative with a burning religious fervor.

We see articles churned out by some prevailing socially-accepted politics publications urging readers to go with their feelings instead of facts. While 'facts don't care about your feelings' may be an attractive mantra to individuals burdened by those to resemble the NPC meme, it's an ineffectual slogan since most rely on their emotions over reason. Most individuals don't read books, but keenly imbibe the Narrative Complex' content. Narratives are facts in themselves even though they don't correlate with reality in itself. The narrative's facts are valorized and cherished by many and evoke an emotional response when threatened. It is my observation that many adherents of prevailing socially-accepted politics do not have children, do not believe in God, and despise their nation's history. The Narrative Complex has become the logos to the prevailing socially-accepted politics which they have deified. To the stereotypical NPC caricatured by the meme, when their worldview is questioned, it isn't like saying something relatively harmless such as "I prefer Pepsi to Coke", but it's a denial of their reality; a sort of blasphemy that insults their very identity. Traditions—such as faith, nation, family—are a kind of received history, and, in adopting the worldview of the prevailing socially-accepted politics, traditions must be excised leaving the individual to renounce their history, becoming tabula rasa, in a manner of speaking. By renouncing their received history—due to interminable propagandizing by the Narrative Complex—what stands in the way of the abyss? Nothing. They can't go back to Christianity.

A family would be difficult to form. Their nation did naughty things 6 generations ago. They'd lose their friends and everything they've emotionally invested into for a large portion of their lives. They've gone all-in. If called, they'd be drawing dead. Their only recourse then would be to leave the table and to collect their winnings.

Even a mainstream outlet such as the Daily Mail, which, sometimes clumsily, reports on stories outside the purview of the prevailing socially-accepted politics narrative, such as crimes committed by migrants or the anti-white—and escalating—government policies in South Africa, has its own interests to preserve. For the enlighted city-dweller, readers of the Daily Mail are intellectual featherweights, therefore, their opinions are automatically invalidated. Not only is there something wholly wrong with those who're of a different opinion, but they're also morally wayward and deserve no more treatment than a barrage of meaningless epithets for their contemptible beliefs.

Whatever negative emotion response is directed at wrongthinkers is neatly wrapped into trendy buzzwords. The idea of intellectual debate, freedom of the press, or a marketplace of ideas is little more than a navel-gazing mirage. Even on social media, there's little political overlap between both political aisle.

Narrative Complex: Triangle of Academia, Entertainment, News Media

The Narrative Complex is the (Bermuda) triangle of Academia, Entertainment, and Mainstream Media. Academia is the breeding ground for many exams forming the prevailing socially-accepted politics, while the Entertainment weaves these politics into their narratives, and the Mainstream Media gives them incrementally favorable exposure. Many of intellectual works which have been quasi-canonical to the prevailing socially-accepted politics were born in an irruption of radical social change in the 60s directly after the most wholesomely-viewed decade, the 50s. Most of these ideas were to relieve oneself from the angst of conforming to outdated and oppressive Western traditions. The answer: unbridled social liberalization. The result: unbridled hedonism, self-deification, solipsism, relativism, and loss of collective self-confidence. The Entertainment industry had been itching to shoehorn more hedonistic narratives into their storylines for years before the emergences of the multitude of liberalizing movements in the 60s.

Shortly after the 60s, the Entertainment narratives shifted from being Americo-centric to Globalistic, promoting alternative forms of contemporary social arrangements which were on the ascendancy. The Mainstream Media clearly paints a narrative through obfuscation, distraction, confusion, and withholding facts. The Mainstream Media manufactures consent, shapes feelings, becomes something of a moral beacon in the sea of relativity formed by tearing down the dams of tradition by Academia and the Entertainment Industry. Academia has access to the brightest and best—tomorrow's leaders—and an opportunity to sculpt their intellectual formation however they deem fit. The brightest and best go off to lead tomorrow's institutions, major corporations, etc, after being steeped in Academia's socially engineering propaganda. The brightest and best are often conscious of their superior intelligence, and, slowly but surely, the ideas promoted by academia are thenceforth associated with higher intelligence. Individuals are stimulated by a pleasant dopamine secretion when they make it known their beliefs coincide with the intelligentsia, despite being ignorant of the fraudulence of these ideas. A whole epistemological system is constructed around unreality. Entertainment and advertising represent a narrative which doesn't coincide with reality itself, as contradicting the prevailing socially-accepted politics narrative would yield a drop in revenue. All three institutions are interrelated in misdirecting, misguiding, and creating valueless individuals whose priorities are inverted. Living for today only matters as there's no tomorrow. The past is problematic, your values cannot be constructed from a problematic and intolerant past which excludes X, Y, and Z minority groups. Your future is beholden to the constantly changing values imposed from above; that is, from the Narrative Complex—your new Logos.

The Narrative Complex self-polices to ensure conformity and ideological purity. Academics and actors will be blacklisted for holding incorrect views. Their presence sows seeds of uncertainty within the prevailing socially-accepted politics. Corporations and the State alike funnel funds to the Narrative Complex to protect their status, scratching each other's backs. A mutual system that assures the oligarchical order's longevity. The Narrative Complex manufactures support for the prevailing socially-accepted politics state, instills a will-to-gratification via the promotion of materialism while being simultaneously supported by the State through funding and corporations through advertisement or the creation of job positions that mandatorily require university education. Life experiences are the best way to avoid the propaganda amplified by all three heads of the Narrative Complex. Corporations and the prevailing socially-accepted political State require individuals to be dwelling within their orbit—being plugged into the system. In order to rule in a modernized world with decentralized technology and the instantaneous transfer of information, the nature of power must evolve to suit such a secular humanist world where those with access to social media are somewhat informed. If the use of power is brutal, as it was in many 20th Century dictator-ships, these structures are easy to identify but they have to rule by the use of fear, which requires constant energy and maintenance of reputation. Ruling through fear in the 21st century—although making a comeback through the threat of imprisoning social media wrongthinkers—would be shambolic due to the rapid spread of infor-mation. If the populace can be kept subject to rule, not by fear, but adoring consent, then a stronger and stabler power structure is formed. Consumer goods and marketable cult-of-personality political figureheads are used to manufacture such adoring consent. Attention spans must be kept low, and time preferences high, to preserve such a political edifice.

By employing and promoting a crazed will-to-gratification, time preferences can be kept high through the use of incentive structures which socially and materially reward adherents to the prevailing socially-accepted politics and consumers. Consuming a certain brand sends a message in a diverse society of rehomogenized blank slates, bereft of identity, as a commodified identity in itself to replace previous identities such as nation or faith. All previous sentimental ties must go. In its place, you can loudly and proudly shout your preferred brands, spread your support for these brands on social media, but don't you dare seek a higher purpose.

Academia:
We've all seen the footage of apoplectic students throwing tantrums at right-of-far-left speakers arriving at their colleges. But where did they form their devout beliefs? From a young age students have become infantilized. They've never been told "no". They simply cannot deal with rejection. They have little-to-no experience with things not going their way. Going back to the amygdala, the highly emotional response could be generated by the fact that their amygdala hasn't adequately developed through an absence of adversity. The information provided by the non-prevailing socially-accepted political speakers at university reveal themselves as an affront to their cushy reality. Much of these

apoplectic tantrums thrown are a result of extreme emotional responses, like a child, used to get what they want; a stifled emotional maturity; and an inability to deal with the concern that the prevailing socially-accepted politics may not coincide with reality itself—because the prevailing socially-accepted politics sound nicer than reality itself.

Entertainment:

All too many shows portray the reverse of the idyllic family-oriented image of 1950s America. The traditional nuclear family is now an unpolished relic of an oppressive age; within a father-mother traditional nuclear family, the father is portrayed as a useless dolt, but the mother is an overworked and unfulfilled heroine; the know-it-all children intellectually outrank their parents—especially the father; it's now "cool" to live a hedonistic life in your early adulthood; religion is only for unthinking, gullible, prudes; before you finally settle down—if you really must!—it's desirable to sleep with as many people as you can get your hands on before you do. And so on and so forth. But the important thing is to avoid thinking about your future.

Many are expected to lead lives way beyond their own potential, which leaves them destitute and miserable. All the narratives portrayed by everyone's favorite shows all glorify having high time preferences. The incentive structure is clear: your peers will revere you more if you live for today, you'll be socially rewarded for living in such a way. Living a high-flying life, as shown by your favorite actors, will satisfy you to no end.

Life is short, and it has to be lived today. Tomorrow may never come, so why think about it? The entertainment industry has trendized a life of permanent adolescence. Adulting is hard and should be strictly limited. Anyway, adults—especially old white ones—tend to be racist bigot partypoopers—you'd hope to never turn into one. You'd do anything in your power to do whatever you can to avoid becoming a hellbound Hitler in your golden years.

> *'Give me a child until he is 7 and I will show*
> *you the man.'*

Many people haven't lived a life—they've lived a narrative. They've lived a narrative which hasn't cared about their wellbeing. They've lived a narrative which has ignored reality because it's a certain time in human history—the current year—and must be unquestioningly accepted, due to our chronological level of enlightenment. They've lived a narrative instead of a life to become guinea pigs for a nefarious social experiment which as converted them into pawns for a political cause. We get the government we deserve. It was her (Hillary Clinton's) turn. As part of living the narrative, self-criticism or self-reflection is made impossible by empowering slogans and in transferring your shortcomings onto despised demographics—that pesky old white male you've been lured into disliking a little. In order for one to maintain a life where time preferences are low, self-criticism and self-reflection are entirely necessary. Trial and error are fundamental to self-improvement. But it's ok, you're perfect just the way you are. Don't let an old white male tell you otherwise.

Imagine being raised in a modern alternative family structure, shuttled off to daycare instead of nutured in their formative years, taken to schools which strive to mould instead of educate, go off to universities swarming with politically-driven professors, watching the TV whose shows and news outlets in their down time that spin narratives celebrating their modern upbringings as progressive and pitting them against their parents for being backwards, if they're loving—heaven forbid. Then, one day, the President of their country is the living embodiment of everything the TV and education system has wholeheartedly condemned as a tyrant—a man who's on the very cusp of recreating the genocidal horrors of the first half of the last century. Or, imagine that we could all live in perfect harmony, be understanding and caring to one another, but there are these backwards individuals who still have the franchise who vote against and hold beliefs contrary to the morally just world you yearn to usher in. How would you feel? Would you think that there's time, in your reality, to sit back and to allow for the morally repugnant people to influence politics or society? Lives are on the line. They must be saved—NOW.

The Narrative Complex constructs a reality which has nothing to do with reality, for politico-economic ends. Denigrating former values and erecting new ones based around a living-for-today and live-and-let-live sloganized philosophy. What life are you to live? You're inundated by choices. When overwhelmed by choice, choice where a purchase is to be made; most shy away from making a purchase as their ability to make a sound value judgement is clouded by a lack of a priori experience and how to successfully apportion their desires. A life of inner conflict, bombardment by choice, and morals being forged by morally unsound individuals chasing after power sounds hellish—because it is.

People are living inauthentic lives where their received history is intercepted by counterveiling narratives, pursuing impossible ends which leads them to nothing but dissatisfaction. Somebody who is satisfied, content with life and their current choices, has no need for a Pied Piper salesman who sells placebos as panaceas. In order to change one's values, information has to change. Information is encrusted with value. With not prior values, new information acts like an anchored floating platform in the rough ocean of relativism.

A reality which has nothing to do with reality.

Politics is immediate gratification—you're awarded dopamine hits for being woke and virtue signalling. Another element to upholding the prevailing socially-accepted politics is the element of righteousness attached to preaching the prevailing socially-accepted politics as gospel. By courageously reaffirming the prevailing socially-accepted politics word, its adherent will be rewarded by a spiritually warming dopamine hit for the virtue signal. Virtue signaling is like cocaine by rewarding the user with a whack of dopamine. But it's also addictive. It requires greater doses and the original experience is impossible to relive. It is also addictive. The overuse of virtue signaling becomes the opposite: a vice. And like an addiction, there's no room for low time preferences in relieving cravings. The demand curve is inelastic. A hit is needed. Becoming further entrenched in prevailing socially-accepted politics is necessary to prolong the virtue signaling addiction. Moreover, cocaine is expensive, but virtue signaling can be done anywhere, at zero cost.

Incentive Structure

Information always changes. Nothing that we know is stable, there is no objective truth to the Narrative Complex. Like dandelion seeds carried in the wind, falling wherever we land, only to be uplifted by another bluster of social change. Everything the Narrative Complex does conveys information. The social dynamics of a Hollywood movie emits metanarratives: metanarratives representing how life is to be lived, power structures, hierarchies, and representations of social importance. The peer review process in some departments is seemingly a politicized—how can I put this politely?—circle jerk. The news is unabashedly politicized, on both sides of the aisle, to fit the prevailing socially-accepted political narrative. Western governments are colluding with social media sites to minimize the distribution of so-called fake news, which funnily enough, has seen officials from more than one country ensnared by their own tyrannical laws. Anything outside of the prevailing socially-accepted politics must be extinguished as it presents an existential threat to the integrity of the narrative. If the truth it itself were on its side, then no measures to clamp down on so-called fake news would be necessary since the truth would self-evidently reveal itself to readers. The truth in itself is the eternal thorn in the side of the establishment. Without alternative media sources Trump and Brexit may not have happened.

These political events should never have happened, which indicates that the Narrative Complex hasn't entirely monopolized the narrative. On an individual level, all three heads of the Narrative Complex cerberus collaborate to promote constantly shifting values and information in order to keep the prevailing socially-accepted politics adherent dependent on their word and in a state of presentmindedness for social, political and economic profit maximization.

CHAPTER 6

TECHNOLOGY

WHAT ARE YOU, A LUDDITE? In the modern age, bringing forward arguments against technology will often see the proponent of these ideas ridiculed. Although we've become more progressive and tolerant as a society, our tolerance has led us to close our minds in a godless world where material wealth is king. While billions have been lifted out of poverty through free enterprise, new challenges have arisen. Man's responsibilities have contracted and mutated since the industrial revolution as labor-saving devices have rendered him obsolete in many fields. It's all well and good that we have inherited a world with unprecendented levels of luxury, but what has this done to man himself? His hands now go daintily uncalloused from labor he once perfunctorily performed. He uses his enfeebled brain less and less than before. He finds it less necessary to imbibe thousands of hours of education as it is all there at the push of a button. Likewise, he no longer has to saunter down to the hightstreet shop in his limited free time to buy the latest gadget. No. Now whatever he wants is right there—again—at a push of a button. Technology breeds technology. But to what end? For the unlimited accretion of technology? What will man's sustained obsolescence at the hands of technology do to man? Is technology meant to lift us to the stars? And, then what? Is technology a higher value than oneself?

The upsides of technology ubiquitously speak for themselves, but I'm not here to wax rhapsodically over the marvels ushered in by techology. With the introduction of labor-saving devices, the average person abandons any vigorous physical training after leaving high school, leaving their muscles to woefully weaken. Physical training is painful, tiring, and requires discipline—discipline of which, partly thanks to technology, people have been dispossessed. Also, in realizing one's potentiality in a discipline such as physical training, there is an element of uncertainty: uncertainty in the end result, and a distinct lack of a guarantee in remotely achieving anything one has set out to realize, thus arriving at the gloomy realm of failure—why waste my time, and life, in pursuing something that may not even come to fruition? Why bother? Also, the tremendous growth in technology ignited by the dawn of the Industrial Revolution, which can be argued as being a materialist reaction following the Protestant Reformation, partly since values shifted from the transcendental to the material, and Catholic teachings on usury were lifted. The rise in technology can be attributed to a loss of faith, in Europe, at least. Meanwhile, the technology that has arisen as a result of the Industrial Revolution has blazed the trail for a multiplicity of social microrevolutions due to the speed and availability of information, ability to wire funds, and cheap goods to alleviate stress which, under more economically primitive conditions, would invoke the need for one to rest their stress and fears in a higher power—God. Technology has been the greatest socially revolutionizing force. However, the question remains whether if Europe's faith had not been rocked, would the Industrial Revolution ever taken place?

In essence, technology opened a can—not diet (bad joke, I know)—of worms in a spiritual sense. Technology endows with the ability to live for today and minimize the consequences in doing so. But, in spite of how nice this may sound, it is effectively rendering man's rational faculties obsolete as a computer can shoulder the burden of thinking for oneself, mediating social relations, and to escape from the miserable repetition of modern urban corporate existence.

Technology has undone the instinctive need for discipline to survive, blighting one's resourcefulness and toughness in the face of hardship. Weak or effete men are sometimes termed "snowflakes" or "soyboys" in reference to their delicate nature and self-aggrandized uniqueness. These so-called "snowflakes" are partly the way they are due to the luxurious upbringings they've been afforded by the availability of technology. Tilling a field or working a mine would somewhat harden their flimsy exterior. As a result of the industrial revolution and advancements in medicine, more people are beating curable diseases and surviving infancy, who otherwise may have been too weak to have survived under more basic conditions. These individuals who may not have survived go on to reproduce, living in an environment where conditions are significantly improved by technology, although returning to simpler, more Darwinian, times may prove fatal to their prolonged genetic existence.

The path of least resistance in technology is clear: if I can have X now at the press of a button, why should I spend time toiling over trying to achieve Y? There's no need to. I no longer have to defer gratification. In fact, I'd be a dunce to wait longer than I need to.

The brain, like muscles, atrophy and wither without stimulation or resistance. Again, after leaving high school, many individuals engage in no mentally stimulating activities aside from what their employment demands. Technology offers mentally disengaging TV shows to pass the time until having to jockey that desk once more for another soul-crushing day at the office. For many, when offered a choice, with no strings attached, after a day at the office to either watch TV or read a history book for a few hours: how many, dear reader, do you think would choose the latter? Although we have everything there at our fingertips, we're in the process of adapting to the fact that we have more information in one place than at any other time in human history. And, as we often take the path of least resistance, as part of our will to expend less energy, we no longer have the need to take the time in absorbing thousands of pages of information, as it is, right there, at our fingertips. Like physical training, mental training—reading and self-study—requires discipline and time. Most jobs are exhausting. Nobody wants to come home to read a book which hasn't been lionized by the

Narrative Complex. It's easier to watch a show on TV. Plus, being social animals, there's a need to be 'with it'. Watching a show that one's workmates or friends enjoy assures to keep that individual in the loop. Assuming that this hypothetical individual works regular hours they would be unwilling to sacrifice watching a show which earns them a part in a social circle over reading a book none of their peers would care for. And despite various labor-saving devices which have bestowed man with unthinkable luxuries, many still spend most of their waking hours on work; limiting available others on other pursuits which would involve summoning discipline, such as the gym. Training mind and body has to transcend the personal value ascribed to unwinding vapid entertainment. Unfortunately, vapid entertainment offers a social benefit and an escape from a mundane job.

Discipline, or power of will, is a form of life force. Discipline, like muscles and mind alike, needs to be trained. Without a purpose to summon a formidable power of will, such as a pregnancy urging a woman to quit smoking or a pencil pusher with a paunch running a marathon for a charity which serves an end close to their heart; discipline is something that must be built over time. Sadly, it requires a little discipline to jumpstart the car of discipline. All too many fall at the first hurdle when undertaking a challenge that requires discipline, due to a weak will and availability of their vice or substitute for their goal—both usually tarted up with a flurry of well-concocted excuses for their dismal shortcomings. It's easier and less time consuming to glibly dismiss one's failures with excuses, especially as, a lot of the time, nobody will chastise one for their failure due to social indifference masquerading as tolerance, and positive reinforcement of the negative by being nice as an excuse for one's lack of self-respect stemming from an uncertainty in one's purpose or identity. Instead of even dishing out positive reinforcement, they are maternally comforted. Being judgemental is now frowned upon. The judgemental person could be on the receiving end of judgement from their peers—for being too judgemental—which can carry a social sentence of ostracism or exclusion. Funnily enough, exclusion and discrimination, in our progressive age, are often deemed unforgivable sins, yet those who wish to look out for their peers in criticizing their waywardness, are considered worse than their ill-disciplined chum. The lack of judgement in our live-and-let-live society isn't a form of caring or trying to let one "be", but is a cheaply disguised form of indifference. Champions of social permissiveness often try to associate their credo with love, understanding, and nurture; but, as I have already stated, their philosophy towards others comes across as indifference—a lack of emotion, a denial of existence. Hatred at least recognises the agency and existence of a person in question, indifference doesn't recognize the person as even worth diverting the minutest momentary care.

Life is short and having to squander one's precious time—a fraction of their life, no less—for aims that may never be realized is foolish, when you have everything you need right there. What's more satisfying than girating between production and sweet, sweet, consumption. You need to assiduously apportion your life and trim out any time that might be wasted which don't derive you any superficial pleasure. Technology has robbed many of the ability to conceptualize personal success. Yes, there are innumerable self-help guides and motivational speakers on the internet; but, don't forget, they themselves are out there pursuing their own ends (profit, fame, etc). Technology has planted itself as an irreplaceable tool for everyday life; without it, people reach an impasse, even if they have manual tools at their disposal to complete the required task. An increased specialization via an ever-expanding division of labor has rendered many city dwellers useless for much DIY, so, they'd much rather call "The Guy". Why wait, acquire new skills, or sweat bullets for a task that "The Guy" can do for a reasonable price and who can be summoned at the touch of a button? It makes no sense. Every hardship has been commodified, but has it really been for one's benefit. The individual's potentiality and faculties have been severely hampered by the commodification of most tasks which get in the way of one's pleasure, and thus, one's ability to consume; although they are, in fact, consuming in relieving themselves of whichever displeasure necessitates them to call 'The Guy'. Under more natural conditions, one would find themselves in a tricky situation as they would be utterly incapable of fending for themselves. In becoming a consumer, a little bit of their humanity has been left behind. Skills which would've been viewed as second nature merely a few generations ago, have fallen by the wayside. Although technology has unquantifiably improved the lives of millions, the individuals abilities have adjusted accordingly, becoming somewhat dependent on technology, as if hooked up to a life support machine.

Great civilizations, before they fall, tend to reach a state of luxury that can only be dreamed of by uncivilized peoples. Ironically, this is often one of the sources to their ultimate demise. Luxury, wealth, and technology often draw in peoples who aren't of the civilization's founding stock. Slowly, but surely, the values, customs, and culture begins to erode until the founding values are ousted or alien. Moreover, as technology rids many of inglorious chores and wealth attracts foreigners to either perform menial tasks far above any realistic wage in their homeland or to simply live parasitically off the fat of the land; the founding stock weakens and becomes more presentminded in order to satiate their unassailable material needs. They, as a whole, cannot wait for new technology to be built with higher domestic wages thus lowering the resources to be funneled toward reinvestment. At the end of civilization, the creation of material wealth—which obviously requires technology—becomes a form of "chasing the dragon", transforming into a tragic flight of Icarus, partly due to the inability of facing the displeasure of deferring gratification as it wouldn't make sense to defer gratification far into a future your kin weren't destined to inherit.

With technology and society set up to preclude responsibilities through the unrivalled luxury and social liberalization we enjoy, man himself becomes a lesser being. The necessity to defer gratification, which requires sustained intelligence, foresight, sacrifice, and purpose; becomes significantly reduced. In many cases, the apple doesn't fall far from the tree; so what will happen to future generations—who are already being brought up fused to their gadgets—when their abilities are almost irretrievably stunted by their unshakable reliance to technology? Cartoons and jokes about how cities have become zombified due to its inhabitants having their eyes glued to their phones, or, how phones have disrupted social occasions. Technology in these respects have most certainly removed something from our being and reduced our quality of personal being. The scope of what we know and do has been reduced due to our reliance on technology. Our freedoms have been trampled on by profit-motivated corporations looking to form consumer profiles or assist with government surveillance. We no longer fully appreciate our families and friends as much as before. Being on the phone while at an event implies a cordial disinterest in said event. One would rather be on the phone, communing with whoever, than at wherever they are. However, what's the guarantee that they wouldn't be on the phone if they were actually with the people they were initially communing with over the phone? It takes time to form bonds and relations. Time has been taken in order to go to such social gatherings. Due to our high time preferences—our inability to defer gratification—we're half-heartedly being with our friends and families. Some have taken measures banning electronic devices at family events or other social gatherings to prevent their usage, to bring back an air of authenticity as we've plugged ourselves into a reality than isn't our own. We've placed our temporal enjoyment above family and community in fixing our eyes on the screen. Technology is replaceable, family isn't. Technology acts as a distraction from what is important. Values become rearranged to squeeze in the enjoyment derived from technology and the possibility of socializing with multiple individuals at once. However, this cannot constitute fully being with family, friends, or community, as concern and energy are expended with others. Discipline is required to voluntarily avoid glancing over at one's phone at a social event. As it is so commonplace, it is acceptable to not fully grant one's full attention to a social situation. There are no real consequences in doing so.

If you don't make time for others, your time will surely run out before you know it. Instead of serving humanity, technology has become something of an end in itself. Technology enables one to fit more opportunities for gratification in one's life. Thanks to technology, the Narrative Complex has been able to diffuse its narratives to deconstruct Western values. Notwithstanding technology gifting the Narrative Complex the means by which it could metastasize within the consciousness of Westerners, technology has also been a double-edged sword for the Narrative Complex. Counterveiling ideas to those of the Narrative Complex have been able to gain traction and disrupt the Narrative Complex' political agenda, culminating in Trump, Brexit, and myriad other populist movements. Thanks to technology, public trust in the Narrative Complex has irrevocably declined. Technology giveth progress life, technology taketh it away.

Metapolitics of Time Preferences

Although an imperfect qualifier, time preferences can, with some observable degree of success, presuppose the politics of an individual. To put it bluntly, high time preferences can be associated with the political left, low time preferences with the political right. However, in many instances, this isn't absolutely correct. On the whole, policies related to high time preferences are traditionally found on the left. *Footnote: I say traditionally because the modern right has become indistinguishable, at least materially, in many ways, to the left. Most people's views aren't anywhere near accurately represented by party politics.* And, low time preferences are generally to be found on the right. For several generations, the left has embodied a spirit of change, revolution, progress, and enlightenment, peaking in the civil rights movement of the 60s and 70s. Within the civil rights movements came women's and sexual liberation, a widespread revolt against traditions, and a spike in the consumption of psychoactive drugs. All three aforementioned social events can be linked to high time preferences: sexual liberation deferring to your carnal impulses with multiple partners with whom no emotion bond has been forged; a revolt against Western traditions and the family both of which require discipline and low time preferences to uphold; the consumption of psychoactives in altering with the state of reality to kill boredom and to bring about a quasi-transcendental state of mind in the face of the death of God. *Footnote, I realize I must sound like a tremendous bore, but, as somebody not unfamiliar with this scene, please save me your speeches about experiences—you're just bored.*

The Image of Somebody with High Time Preferences

Having low time preferences appears to be boring and repetitive. The media portrays old right-wingers as disconnected from reality, uncool, and bigoted, which has become something of a meme. But, with a goal or goals in mind, low time preferences can become more rewarding. Fulfillment can be found in discipline and sacrifice. Discipline and sacrifice aren't typically behaviors of a hedonist; in fact, quite the opposite. A life lived fast rarely harvests much satisfaction. Standing among one's peers living life to the best of one's ability and becoming something of a role model in how to approach one's time. And role models of a more traditional bent are represented as dull, racist, or secretly perverted by the Narrative Complex. The role models we're now treated to are quite the opposite. They can do it all. They often haven't made their wealth by working long, hard hours. They often don't spend much time as a family. Many have a penchant for drink. Others are philanderous. Before the civil rights era, our modern role models or heroes would be considered unfit for polite society, let alone elevated to such revered positions. There's a lack of judgement of one's foibles. We like to avoid

conflict at all costs. One thing judgement is, is consequence. If you live or act in a certain way, your peers
will judge you for it. You, provided you have no mental
defects, should feel guilt. Guilt, being a powerful tool,
should prevent you from living or acting in a certain
way again in the future. Social policing of this nature is
becoming a thing of the past. Ironically, you'll see
individuals, who are probably atheistic, with tattoos
scribbled with 'only God can judge me'. Judgement presupposes superiority. In a very egalitarian age, regardless of status, wealth, or achievement, nobody is fit to
judge. The reality is that nobody likes guilt—or consequences. An absence of judgement is another form of
infantilization, delaying discipline. And, with time, it'll
only get worse for the individual who's been bereft of
judgement. There could be life-changing consequences
when they're hit with real judgement, such as prison or
worse.

On the one hand, role models have been removed
from the fray, giving no guidance as to how one should
lead one's life—especially in broken homes or where a
father is absent—and, on the other hand, nobody is
perceived to be socially fit to judge the actions of those
brought up without an adequate role model. They have
been thrown into a world where they are doomed to
forever sail on a tempestous ocean with no shore in sight
and no anchors on board. They lack a personal authenticity as who they are doesn't necessarily match with the
media narratives. They are told they are X, when, in
actual fact, upon some personal reflection, may turn out
to be Y. They are urged to lead lives which may not

necessarily be possible to uphold as they strive to exceed their limits in order to conform to certain artificial social expectations. An extreme example of this would be somebody claiming that they identified as a dog: they can mimic a dog's behavior, dietary habits, and lifestyle, but they aren't authentically a dog although they wish to live as one. This is, of course, an extreme example of the inauthenticity I wish to convey, but approaching time preferences is made more challenging if one attempts to pursue an inauthentic lifestyle.

Lifting weights is a potential marker for low time preferences as there's a potential goal in mind, discipline is essential, repetition, sacrifice, and pain are almost daily, but the rewards are great. Sometimes, gymgoers work arduously for years earning no sizable gains. A few humorously-worded studies and articles have shown how physically stronger men are likelier to espouse right-wing views unlike their scrawnier counterparts. Weight training is also associated with higher levels of testosterone which is associated with higher aggression (not passive-aggression), competitiveness, and masculinity. Militaristic levels of discipline and pain tolerance are traditionally associated with masculinity. Less agreeableness, or, as I like to call it, "the ability to say no", is also a trait aligned with masculinity. Taking responsibility is associated with 'manning-up'. Traits which are crucial to having low time preferences—duty, responsibility, discipline, and sacrifice—in large part, could be associated with masculinity, which is associated with right-wing politics. There is, therefore, a metapolitical case to be made suggesting that, on the whole, low time preferences is associated with being right-leaning.

Paradoxically, however, is the alliance of the super wealthy with left-wing politics, seeing as wealth creation is often associated with intelligence and low time preferences. However, pro-Establishment politics offers lobbyists and the wealthy alike to push through social engineering policies which favor their short and long term success. Furthermore, prevailing socially-accepted politics adherence resembles religiosity rather than political support. Tremendous wealth not only commands money-power in politics, but also elevates the wealthy donor into a demigodlike position of power. Additionally, many of the super wealthy have been educated at top universities, remaining in likeminded cliques imbued in Narrative Complex narratives who unwaveringly espouse the same beliefs given their social disconnection to the hoi polloi. Despite their potential lower time preferences than the average Joe, they are able to rig the game to their own long term gain, leading to their espousal of pro-Establishment, prevailing socially-accepted politics-dictating positions.

The cruel irony here is that only those with pre-ordained with the prevailing socially-accepted politics are fit to pass judgement on the rest of us. The nature of this judgement isn't correctional, but punitive. It only metes out punishment. If you dwell outside its orbit, you can stand to have your name forever tarnished, lose your source of income, be silenced for your malicious wrongthink, and even have your freedom revoked. What's worse is that those indoctrinated by the prevailing socially-accepted politics, despite their egalitarian fantasies, have arrogated to themselves an ascended level of self-importance. Judgement, as I've said, presupposes superiority. They've contradictorily allowed themselves to believe in the divine supremacy of their views while simultaneously preaching equality. This must be an agonizing source of cognitive dissonance.

CHAPTER 7

THE DEATH OF HEROISM

OLDER SOCIETIES WOULD PASS DOWN—albeit in many cases, implausible—myths and stories of their heroes who mustered superhuman strength, energy, and will to accomplish amazing things. As many myths have been debunked as unrealistic, the baby has been throw out with the bath water killing off the memory of the hero. Heroes may have died, but the need for a hero, even in our modern rational society, still exists. This hero, however, is not of a similar transcendental nature. Heroes such as great military leaders, writers, artists, statesmen, etc, have been denigrated by the prevailing anti-Western sentiment amplified by the Narrative Complex. The reality the Narrative Complex paints is one where former heroes aren't worth celebrating, demoralizing the individual to the point where they loathe their history; and consequently, themselves. Old heroes are simply being replaced with new ones. Today, a hero MUST have the establishment-approved politics, otherwise they are tossed aside. The hero today must excel in a spiritually unimportant field such as sport, popular music, or cinema. These heroes often lead hedonistic and self-destructive lifestyle. Millions wish to purchase their fashion, products, and lead similar lifestyles. Actors and sportsmen are revered, as long as they don't have the wrong politics, even if they're abusive to their spouses, consume illicit drugs, commit adultery, and lead a flashy and unsustainable lifestyle. The media and entertainment industry lionizes those who toe the party line despite their sordid actions. Those who live more wholesomely are mocked and black-balled. The modern hero lives a life of high time preferences. These are the people who are to be emulated. But, is there any public figure, by older standards, who'd have a statue made after their lives?

Before the 20th century, heroes often resembled something that would be despised by modern standards: disciplined, driven, unrelenting, responsible, and willing to put a cause greater than oneself as a higher goal. Somebody who could stand above their peers is often shot down in an egalitarian fury. In a more commodified world, business and wealth has become a yardstick for social achievement. Nationalism is a dirty word. Former heroic statesmen would be considered backwards by an application of today's lowly standards. Heroism is at odds with social egalitarianism. However, the men and women who are looked up to lead vapid and empty lives. The Narrative Complex promotes these individuals to create a more materialistic society—one that is geared towards consumption. Rap music, in particular, is elevated and recognized as being "cool". Many rap lyrics are centered around promiscuity, the aimless accumulation of resources, violence, drugs, and getting one's drink on. These lyrics celebrate a lifestyle based around succumbing to one's whims. Many pop songs, although not implicitly promoted as cool, convey a similar yet dampened message.

For many, it's a case of monkey see, monkey do: if the Narrative Complex' figureheads are devolving into a more primitive state, one that has lost control of its impulses, lives for the moment: how will most decide to live their lives? It simply isn't trendy to have low time preferences. This is a bores's business. Only a party pooper would rather blow off steam by reading a book, listening to a podcast, or working out—it simply ain't cool. And a life of low impulses breeds politics which prolong and enhance such a lifestyle. Advocating for policies which can enable living in a state of unreality are manifested in such things like abortion in removing the consequences of care-free unprotected sex; child benefits for if the man who knocks you up is an unstable provider; healthcare in removing/externalizing the consequences of living an unhealthy lifestyle such as obesity, drug abuse, binge drinking, unprotected sex, etc; welfare for if you chose a worthless degree, kept no savings, or recklessly lost your job; and whole other plethora of socially-acceptable lifestyles which come at both a tremendous financial and social cost. Many of these social programs which have been twisted by some to accommodate fast living were introduced by traditionally left-wing politicians; pushed by academics, journalists, and movie directors; and redrafted the West's moral blueprint to demonize those against unlimited social liberalization, rendering any opponents of the new moral virtues as moral outsiders.

The socio-political programs which support high time preferences have become political mainstays in the current climate as attempts to undo these programs would be inglorious political suicide. However, given the strange evolution of left-wing politics since the civil rights era shifting away from protecting the working class towards a more globalist, bourgeois, hedonist, structuralist, and ultra-subjectivist demeanor; instead of exclusively protecting the interests—or claiming to protect the interests—of the most economically vulnerable and socially immobile, their leadership seems to have embraced a turbo-charged acceleration down a track of promoting low-impulse control and a consequence-free living-for-today philosophy. Somebody else will pay for it. Dressing up a wafer-thin rationale in meandering post-structuralist verbiage as to why it's not only necessary, but deserved. Historical wrongs are to be amended. The nuclear family has been a fetter to the liberation of the individual—irrespective of age or sex. The wealthy, even if their fortune was made via painstaking hard work and legitimately provided a good or a service to the betterment of society, are the reason why you can't enjoy a luxurious life of pleasure—fully automated luxury gay space communism with eternal cummies, so to speak.

FOOTNOTE: *Of course—and I must stress this—not all individuals dependent on social programs are in such a situation by fault of their own; I merely wish to highlight that there exists a metapolitical incentive structure to enable high time preference lifestyles where it's become almost trendy to call for additional social programs to facilitate an unproduc-*

tive and libertine existence.

We often hear how old white men have been the direct result of all our social ills—rather ageist, racist, and sexist if you ask me. In Britain, young voters have excoriated old pro-Brexit voters for ruining their country when they will be dead. Although many of the politically vocal young wish to paint themselves out as being progressive and egalitarian, there's an intense hatred for the elder stereotype who may embrace more reactionary politics. Full of youthful energy and further energized by the existence of inequalities, inequities, and suffering which, by cunning linguistic sleights of hand, has diverted the blame onto a demographic which will be slowly phased out over time. The future is now, old man. Like a semi-Peter Pan-esque state, many young political activists who live fast don't seem to realize that age will catch up to them. If they have a family, their views may evolve with their change social status. They may become the geriatric reactionary who they so viciously despised in their early adulthood; those dreadful old people who stubbornly prevented them from ushering in a utopia. But what undergirds this resentment towards the politically-active elderly is high time preferences and a trans-generational gap in information. Many of the elderly voters grew up before the Civil Rights movement. Many were taught to believe in their nation's sovereignty, before the Narrative Complex corrupted our mindsets. It's high time preferences to want to undo a society which took centuries to build. It's a profound lack of wisdom and hubris to believe that a better world can be midwived by those who've barely finished puberty, once all the old people have met their maker.

Wisdom takes time to form. Wisdom takes experience. Wisdom takes consequence. Somebody who lives fast may profess wisdom, but is that wisdom authentic when it isn't applied to their daily lives? High time preferences coupled with technology that bestows us with an unprecedented wealth of knowledge at our fingertips spells entitlement. If somebody's wisdom doesn't match up to the prevailing socially-accepted politics is automatically discredited. In fact, if somebody's achievements don't match up to the prevailing socially-accepted politics, their achievements are automatically discredited. This is a revolt against wisdom, an inability to entertain an opposing viewpoint. Here, an opposing viewpoint isn't simply a differing perspective, but an affront or a personal attack. Some have willy-nilly imbued themselves with the prevailing socially-accepted politics to the extent where anything dwelling outside its orbit is downright illegitimate. Cutting people out of one's life, such as family members, for having the wrong views takes low impulse control or high time preferences as there may be avoidable long-term consequences in doing so. Discrediting older people on their views alone, instead of calmly attempting to reform their crystallized thoughts takes high time preferences. Some have taken to social media to boast about how their Trump-supporting racist uncle was epically pwned by their enlightened cousin who's a feminist second-year anthropology student. When it comes to family, conflict is best avoided for stronger bonds and a healthier relationship. Entering a shouting match over clashing views isn't beneficial in the long term. Low time preferences means that pride is swallowed or unpleasant people are stomached in the short term for long-term harmony. Conflict is best avoided through reason and acting peacefully where necessary to preserve familial or social ties. Sadly, across generations, there is an utter disconnect in information and values. Modern values from political correctness to consumerist atomization have led to a disconnection between succeeding generations, where received history and intepretation of truth for newer generations is radically different to that of older generations—in a way, erasing their past, converting them into a blank slate, of sorts.

The received information between the elderly and young adults are almost alien to one another. In between, lies the middle-aged parent who was raised during the Civil Rights Era which could be seen as a radically transitional phase between a dying conservative nationalism and a burgeoning post-national, technocapitalist, relativist age. Information and social perception of alternative lifestyles have never, in human history, changed so abruptly. And it won't be without intense repercussions.

Low time preferences are needed to will to preserve a nation: indifference and high time preferences will do quite the opposite. By deferring gratification beyond one's own life to bequeath to one's ancestors a healthy, stable, and secure society is priceless. A secure and, in a sense, relatively homogenous social unit by necessity requires social conservatism. Everything begins with the family and the rest follows. It's no accident that the greatest waves of immigration into Western societies has coincided with the utter collapse of the family unit. If there's nothing greater than oneself to preserve, why preserve it? Behaviors underpinned by high time preferences and incentive structures in place to live accordingly are directly responsible for the dissolution of the nuclear family. With something greater than oneself to preserve—family and nation—many individuals will be less likely to wish to jeopardize these things, which money cannot buy, with cheap and meaningless thrills. By assuming new responsibilities such as a family; values and incentives change. Many middle class British families wish to remain in the European Union as it endows their children with more job opportunities on the continent. The information they have, which is in line with the prevailing socially-accepted politics as most of their information is extracted from the Narrative Complex, dictates that their incentive structure which would be most beneficial to their children is to remain in the EU. They feel that more stability and security can be offered by remaining in this political superstructure. Others wish to reclaim political sovereignty for the ability of their kin to decide for their own future. However, as previously stated, low time preferences correlate with intelligence; and, intelligent people are highly educated in a system which enforces ideological uniformity—the prevailing socially-accepted politics. In essence, individuals can only make decisions—long and short term—based on the information they have— whether objectively right or wrong. Smart people can be conned into having high time preferences if all the knowledge they have indicates the virtues of living accordingly. Likewise, intelligent people can have low time preferences without a moral and epistemological framework dictated by the intelligentsia spearheading the prevailing socially-accepted politics, which, in the case of the EU, unquestionably suggests further political integration towards one world government, to avoid the potential instability of isolationist nationalism in a globalized economy. Ironically, the globalist revolutionary becomes a reactionary to preserve a world, according to their socially-acceptable knowledge, which is optimally desirable. They may be associated with the political left in today's inaccurate left-right paradigm; however, their goals are relatively far-sighted. Order and stability are traditionally associated with right-wing or reactionary politics. Order and stability are foundational to having low time preferences in order to make far-sightedness more possible by minimizing risk or the potential distortion of information in the future.

CHAPTER 8

POLITICS—AND THE POLITICIZATION OF EVERYTHING

TO DENY THAT THE MEDIA and entertaining have allied themselves with political causes would be of either the highest dishonesty or rankest ignorance. Almost all TV shows have a clear political bent to them. Just look at the latest Netflix shows: they are bursting with clear narratives and metanarratives depicting how we should lead our lives in line with a metapolitical incentive structure which assures a certain form of political thinking and voting. The mainstream media—with few exceptions—seem to be little more than glorified well-monied outlets for political activism rather than fearless truthseekers. From leading the charge into foreign wars, to promoting a race-baiting narrative, to brazenly denigrating political candidates and causes different to theirs; both the mainstream media and entertainment industry—although becoming increasingly indistinguishable from one another—unashamedly inject political talking points into their productions. The average Joe often hasn't the time to do thorough research before taking part at election time. Many individuals form their political opinions around fluttering half-truths, their loved ones, or snippets of entertainment shows which, now, instead of portraying a gripping story, represent a political narrative, and counterfeit a 'reality' which doesn't follow reality itself. Trying to emulate these lifestyles or examining the social arrangements on TV will be a cause for inner disharmony. Furthermore, everything, by necessity, must be political. To ensure that Westerners continue to feed from the globalist trough unabated, there has to be a deep emotional investment to the Narrative Complex' narrative. Propaganda must be constant; otherwise cognitive dissonance will set in, thus threatening the narrative's validity. Everything explicitly or implicitly must have a political bent to preserve the authenticity of the inauthentic Narrative Complex narrative. People are rushed to political judgement since no stone has been left unturned by politics, and being apolitical is to be left out of the social loop. Since a new political outcry is amplified by the media every week, there is no stability. Intrinsic to the nature of party politics, all that matters is winning and then solidifying one's position of power thereafter, for as long as possible.

Part of the "politicization of everything"—as I shall call it henceforth—is to seep political narratives and dialectics into the conscience of the unexpecting viewer/consumer. By painting a world untarnished by politics, political thinking thereby becomes inseparable to the most pedestrian of daily tasks. The media and information industry holds a monopoly on language, how language develops and evolves, and on what language must avoided or be considered evil. Certain words such as "gay", "negro", "queer", etc have had their primary meanings change in lockstep with the emergence of civil rights movements. Phrases such as "colored people" is a no-no, but "people of color" is progressive. The quickening instability of words in their meaning makes for a world of eggshells—be careful where you tread! If you were to utter a word now deemed blasphemous... I mean, off-limits, by the information intelligentsia, you may suffer excommunication from, as Moldbug puts it, "The Cathedral". Language and its meanings have changed so rapidly that famous writers such as G.K. Chesterton, Joseph Conrad, Thomas Carlyle, and many others who are still loved today would see their careers evaporate into nothingness and their names indelibly sullied for their liberal usage of the "N-Bomb". The average Joe cannot afford to make such transgressions, and, therefore, would have to tread extremely lightly in order for the egg shells to rest uncracked. The average Joe is mostly aware of the implications of transgressing against the prevailing socially-accepted politics' logos. Most people just want to be left alone. But the prevailing socially-accepted politics's adherents are inquisitional in ensuring conformity.

With party politics and a one-man-one-vote system is that eventually, politics, when a side has little to offer the core demographic, becomes aware that democracy is little more than a demographic headcount. Therefore, if the core demographic cannot be convinced to elect a party on policy alone, then it would be best to promote new groups who will tend to vote more as a block than on an individual basis. This is one of the main reasons as to why there has been a populist reaction. Entire neighborhoods have changed. East London in many places, for example, isn't the tough Dickensian working class scenery of yesteryear. But if you notice—let alone, dislike—the transformation of the place your grandparents grew up in, then there's something pathologically and morally dysfunctional in you. There will be consequences for your noticing. You could lose it all. So, shut up, consume, watch your TV, and keep your head down.

Language has always evolved. But now, it seems, we are approaching something akin to terminal velocity. When language changes so rapidly, the meaning of things becomes somewhat obscured, devalued, denatured. When the meaning of language evolves at warp speed, truth becomes unmoored since the language backing it constantly shifts. Constructing values or even understanding becomes challenging when language and phrases, in particular, shed their meaning according to fleeting social norms and trends. Decades ago, the word 'queer' was acceptable. Suddenly, it was unacceptable. Now, it's not only acceptable, but lauded to denote empowerment among certain groups. Part of the trouble concerning politics and the drifting meaning of words is that adherents of the prevailing socially-accepted politics are presented with intellectual members of the establishment promoting policies which may not be in the adherents best long term interest. However, an adherent may not want to challenge their beliefs as an intellectual superior from the establishment uttered something conflicting with the adherent's long-term interest. Furthermore, those outside of the prevailing socially-accepted politics are maligned as 'racists', 'dullards', 'uneducated', etc—why would they want to believe something the scourge of the university may believe? In accepting politics promoted by the Narrative Complex, the adherent can also discover self-confidence in their beliefs being aligned with the brightest and best the universities have to offer. Prevailing socially-accepted politics' adherents can gleefully accept policies which go against their long-term interests as long as the prevailing socially-accepted politics intelligentsia and Narrative Complex were the ones to craft these ideas. They'd be stupid not to.

Only bigoted knuckle-dragging primitive racists, Republicans, old white men, and their kind could possess an alternative vision of how the world show be. And they're wrong—all the best columnists say that these incrementalist policies will boost GDP! Put simply: smart people vote how the coastal columnists suggest we should; dumb people vote otherwise. Wouldn't wanna be dumb, now, would you? To seek affirmation in one's own intelligence when its everpresent in the Narrative Complex must uplift the spirit. By getting a cushy dopamine hit in unswervingly agreeing with their policies—despite their intentions—the prevailing socially-accepted politics adherent could argue for their own existence to be discarded while simultaneously believing in their own superior intelligence in the process. Almost any policy can be passed through—no matter how ludicrous—as long as agreement for said policy were associated with intelligence. Anything can be passed if all the brainiac talking heads unanimously agree with the policy—regardless of its intentions. Policies promoting high time preferences, which have become undisputable political mainstays—welfare, graduated taxation, inflation, social liberalization, sexual freedom—remain unchallenged as the vast majority of society's intelligentsia agree with them uncritically. Criticism could spell ostracism. Nobody wants to feel dumb or left out. Consent can be manufactured by demonstrating the unanimity of the most intelligent public figures in following a certain political talking point through their promotion in the media.

The current global political order—neoliberalism—is seemingly a political synthesis of: thesis—liberalism— and antithesis—marxism—of a bastardized nature. Neoliberalism checks the materialist or economic boxes of the mainstream left-right dichotomy, although it is fundamentally a progressive, "end of history" doctrine and a self-acclaimed ideal. It has struggled to transcend human nature and individual sentimentality. It talks a tall game, but falls short of the mark in pleasing everyone. The main problem with progress in this regard is that it verges on uncharted territory. For progress to avoid become a strain of conservatism, it cannot rest—it must keep progressing. A perfect world must be in statis, unchanging. But constant change is anathema to low time preferences as values shift according to the increased possibility of new information down the line. Low time preferences need to be rooted in firm ground. Referring to the past offers a great frame of reference in adopting values as they are clearly stated and a conception of the past lives in one's mind, providing a clear image of what to strive for. The actions of great figures and heroes—in spite of storytelling embellishments—offer guidance as to how one should live. Adopting a preference for progress partly requires to keep one's options open, as what we know tomorrow may change; therefore, weakening any present commitment due to their potential future invalidity, which may prompt more presentmindedness in their actions, given the uncertainty of the future.

Time preferences will tend to rise in a society where language shifts. People will bend over backwards in order not to offend. Offense-taking is mostly subjective, but due to the significant power and influence of media and entertainment; offense-taking has become a form of seizing social status. As ridiculous as it may sound, people go to extraordinary lengths in order to avoid offending people, such as: calling somebody by their preferred pronouns if they're non-binary or otherkin, sidestepping culturally-loaded language, decrying one's own history—despite having non ancestors who played a direct role in influencing the course of history or injuring those defeated/colonized—self-effacingly dedicating large portions of one's life to further the ends of differing groups, etc. All these things are done in the name of being an ally, but as numerous outlets of the fringes of the mainstream media denounce: it isn't enough! You should do more for these causes or you're the moral equivalent of a heretic. This is, of course, an extreme form of the narrative set up by the Narrative Complex, in particular, by academia, but, nevertheless, one that has been a direct cause of emotional distress to allies of these causes.

Turn on the TV and you won't be hard-pressed to unearth the narrative du jour. Shows incorporate their narratives with about as much subtletly as a brick to the face. The average Joe often doesn't care much for the narrative, minority groups have their sensitivities inflamed by these provocative narratives. For a while, in America at least, members of The Democratic Party, on TV, are played by gentle, understanding, altruistic, caring, erudite, pleasant, amicable, affable, tolerant winners; whereas Republicans are almost always gun-toting, uncouth, racist, loud, obnoxious, uneducated, crude, mysogynistic, ignorant, jingoistic, retrograde losers. In a world of two party politics, politicking for the uninformed is like a soccer penalty shoot out as a goal keeper; pick a side and choose—but choose correctly: you wouldn't want to be perceived by your peers as the entertainment narrative portrays you now, would you?

The reality is that both party's establishments are as rotten as each other. Neither of them has the nation's best interest at heart. The left imports third-worlders for votes as they've lost the hearts of the nation's working class; the right imports third-worlders for cheap labor under the banner of supporting "free-market" principles. Both parties have cozied up to megacorporations and have hollowed out the pulsating corpse of America—and Western Civilization—for votes, privileges, and payment in the here and now. Even our politicians have high time preferences, demonstated by their questionable lifestyle choices and reckless actions, which we've all got to suffer in the future. But at least they got their's. The age of statue-worthy statesmen is behind us in the materialistic age. Everyone has a price. Everything can be commoditized—even your future! But the transformation to our current materialist political stage where faceless interchangeable political oligarchs, are voted in by faceless interchangeable consuming-producers, to the profit maximization of a small money-power, was a long one. It took generations and unimaginable bloodshed to get to this destination. For politicians, nothing—except for their sponsors—is greater than their egos. They are at the pinnacle of human achievement and you, my friend, are little more than a fungible economic unit whose assigned purpose in life is to make big numbers on a screen even bigger. And don't you dare rock the boat. If you do, your numbers on the screen might vanish. If you live for tomorrow or your children, how will megacorporations cope? They need to sell their worthless dopamine-secretion-inducing products today. The GDP will fall. The stock market will crash. You can't let the megacorporations, who own your politicians and who've sold out your future for present gain, go bankrupt, could you? The current politico-economic climate is a parasitical lifeforce whose host is Western materialism and will-to-gratification. With a little discipline, by ceasing to be a slave to your material desires; the stranglehold will ease its grip. The house of cards is propped up by high time preferences, driven by consumerism.

As a stunning reflection of our age of high time preferences, our politicians often embody society at large. In this case, our politicians don't act for tomorrow, but for today. At the time of writing this, several Western leaders are childless. Some people may shrug their shoulders at this information, but what is their skin in the game? Why should they care what happens to their nations after they expire if they haven't left behind a legacy? Talk is cheap. Politics is dictated by hollow platitudes and big money. There needs to be something more substantial as a guarantee—collateral—to ensure that leaders don't figurative screw the pooch. That is, to say, of course, that not all politicians who are childless don't care about the welfare of their countries once they've left office. Politicians with children often malodorously linger after their time in office to cement their family's stead and to continue to cheerily accept kickbacks from multinationals or other myriad interest groups to protect their political dynasty. The underlying pattern for most globalist politicians is either: 1) no skin in the game—childlessness or 2) protecting their skin in the game—prostituting themselves to major corporate interests.

For the childless politician, it doesn't really matter for his/her country to be flooded by unassimilable, hostile migrants, who, apart from humanity, share nothing in common with the host population. Flourishing as upstanding members of the community isn't a priority, especially as the existing incentive structures—welfare, housing, schooling, anti-racist activists, political correctness, etc—all act as impediments towards any semblance of integration.

Furthermore, since large minorities can put forward

their own political candidates, who, invariably "play the system" in order to command the most resources, laws, rights, perquisites for their own group; questions concerning the legitimacy of a political system, which allows legal elements alien to the founding national stock to become embedded within the nation's laws to benefit hostile minorities, should be made. Once the proverbial hits the fan, the childless politician will either have begun the process of ossification or be heavily guarded in a gated residence. Either way, they don't get to suffer the consequences of their own actions. The other politician with a legacy to protect will work assiduously to ensure their children and grandchildren never feel the consequences of their traitorous actions. The underlying theme appears to be the democratization or socialization of consequences onto others. The populace will feel the brunt of the consequences for impulsive economic and immigration policies—not the politician. It is the working class who have been hardest hit by feel-good, jazzhands, Kumbaya globalism. How else could the spiritual bleakness of the current political landscape be cloaked? How else can millions of voters gingerly follow the neoliberal Pied Piper? A cross between fantastical promises of a prosperous utopian world, and viciously silencing or smearing naysayers, has been the favored ingredient to the neoliberal melting pot. The working class—not city-dwelling elites—have been alienated by deindustrialization and mass immigration. Their communities have been kneecapped by joblessness, crime, addiction, suicide, broken homes— the root causes of which can be, in a large part, attributed to a spiritual decay which has been repackaged as dopamine-secreting feel-good politics promoted by the Narrative Complex.

While I have painted a gloomy picture, we may have been foredoomed by our shoddy political incentive structures. Unfortunately, in a world where everyone can vote, yet little are informed, but many avidly watch television; it's no surprise our political landscape is conditioned such. All the smart people vote a certain way. All the cool celebrities vote a certain way. My favorite brands support all of my favorite political causes. Conversely, all the bad people vote the other way. Those bad people are the ones delaying us from achieving a brighter future. The people who the Narrative Complex warned me about, depicted as malignant, and vilified as atavistic ne'er-do-wells, all support the opposite positions. It's a simple choice, really.

Most Western countries have something resembling a two party system: one party on the center-left, another on the center-right. Society's political views have gradually shifted leftwards since WWII, but have blasted the nitrous oxide since the 1990's. If you're a politician looking to realistically gain power, you must keep all of your increasingly multicultural constituents pleased. This means having to allow social concessions for conflicting groups. If you don't, you must be racist, so yield your station for a more deserving POC. Most of the electorate isn't educated, per se, but have gone through public education which has deprived them of critical thinking skills. Public education, lauded as irreplaceable, serves only as a production line of producing-consumers as a transfusion of new economic activity for an ageing Western world. The Welfare state has also expanded as a result of mass immigration, deindustrialization, and destigmatization. To the corporate-backed politician, immigration is desirable to boosting economic metrics and corporate profitability, as the potential to consume for a migrant from a Third World country— even if they lived exclusively from state welfare—is several times greater than they would be able to back at home.

On the whole, the politician and electorate have forged an unhappy marriage based on high time preferences. Somebody has to pick up the tab. But, as we've previously established, that somebody stuck with the tab is the children the preceding generations forewent. For consequences—the tab—to be valued, they need to concern somebody first. I have a sinking feeling that most who move to a foreign country and saw their tax rates rise because of a debt accrued by a fiscally irresponsible preceding generation, it wouldn't be too graciously received on the part of the newcomer. It ain't my debt, it ain't my problem. People don't want to suffer the consequences of the actions of others. Nobody is that selfless, particularly if it was because of the childishness of their short-term promises for short-term gain. But since all other forms of government have been shown, by history, to have been tried and failed, one-man-one-vote universal suffrage democracy is the only viable political option. Abolishing the current order IS a tall order given the money-interests which necessitate a pacified, consumerist, electorate. However, although history is a catalog of ineffectual, brutal, and violent preceding political orders; none have lead to such profound propagandizing, self-hatred, and misdirection to the point where the electorate was in the process of voluntarily destroying the greatest civilization to have ever existed to appease their own self-hatred and celestially lofty ideals promising to transcend human nature, other than modern neoliberal democracy and the social engineering of the Narrative Complex.

An incentive structure is in place to promise an electorate—made ever more stultified and impatient by the Information Complex's disinformation—more resources and to live an unsustainable lifestyle—a lifestyle which cannot be criticized without a frenzied backlash. It's trendy to glibly dismiss one's foibles with modern verbiage or to shirk blame of one's actions. Manning up is hard in an unmanly world, especially where manhood is demonized as "toxic masculinity"—a line usually parroted by those which have little contact with masculinity, irrespective of their being male or female. People don't like to suffer consequences. They're unpleasant. Owning up is hard. But in a realm of party politics, owning up is self-destructive, loserish. But it's nice when the political structure is set up in such a way that those with the correct politics never get to suffer the consequences of their actions, no matter how base. The same also applies to adherents of this political credo. A multiplicity of warped standards is improvised to justify or conceal certain behaviors. An example of this is how Bill Clinton, Harvey Weinstein, Kevin Spacey, et al, were accused of sexual waywardness but the furore was contained by the media's damage control campaign, but Justice Kavanaugh was flayed by the press for suspiciously improbable accusations that emerged at an opportunistic political moment, then later silently dropped.

In the long run, without the Narrative Complex batting for a certain side, owning up should be considered something honorable. Guilt isn't a pleasant feeling. It can cause emotional pain. But there's many-a cure for that and many-a palliative, but you've just gotta consume. The second one of the bad guys makes a faux pas, it's time to pounce. If one of the good guys makes a faux pas, you accuse the other side of pouncing. See how it works? This is how you're always in the right. You've got to have the mental fortitude to swim against the current. Living a metapolitical life—rejecting consumerism, advocating fitness, advocating low time preferences, promoting family values, distrusting the narrative—is a surefire way to villification, as that person is an existential threat to the narrative. You're always the baddie, even if you make others aware of the Narrative Complex' fallacies, misreporting, and mendacity.

It requires low time preferences to construct a social interrelation and trust worth having. Having to stomach unpalatable individuals to preserve social peace requires curbing one's impulses for future gain in the form of present harmony. Using reason as conflict resolution instead of violence requires foresight to interpret consequences of one's actions. Violence could mean a loss of freedom and even the formation of vendettas.

Reason and negotiation allows one to peacefully acquire resources or cooperation without disrupting the immediate social order. By curbing one's impulses, a potentiality for increased future gain appears through forming reciprocal social bonds. Being pleasant to one's neighbors and communities offers long term benefits, even if the individual isn't naturally pleasant. Understanding the consequences of alienation or the use of violence requires self-reflection, intelligence, and low time preferences. Denting one's reputations through a violent outburst will affect their social standing in the future. High time preferences lowers social trust as immediate personal gain is implied in having high time preferences. On the one hand, the self-deifying consumer has high time preferences in order to consume as a means to fill the void, on the other, the less advanced individual living under harsher conditions has high time preferences as a means to survive.

Corruption—which is seemingly rife in Western politics if one remains skeptical to the Mainstream Media's narrative—is partly a product of high time preferences, with the goal of furthering one's status, wealth, and power often to the detriment of the electorate. Countries which suffer the least political corruption often boast the highest national average IQs. Low time preferences, correlating with intelligence, also seem to correlate with reduced susceptibility to political corruption. That's not, to say, corruption will be absent in highly intelligent societies, but corruption levels should be lower in higher countries. Being corrupt has social consequences: diminished social trust, resources allocated away from infrastructure to back pockets, higher criminality, less justice, and many other socially undesirable effects ensue from high levels of corruption. Few developed countries suffer high levels of corruption. Corruption prevents prosperity from taking flight.

Corruption is wholly decivilizing—as is high time preferences. However, corruption can run amok where the rest of society lives with high-time preferences as present gratification trumps the supposed benefits in future gratification from a healthy, cohesive, and stable society instead of a me-first presentminded consumerist feeding trough. The incentive structure cloaking corruption as an appetizing option to honesty is the fact that the Narrative Complex will protect corrupt politicians to adherents of the prevailing socially-accepted politics who will morally exculpate or cover up the indiscretion of the corrupt politician—provided that the politician represents the prevailing socially-accepted politics. The corrupt politician is shielded from direct consequences from their corrupt actions which allows the to behave so unscrupulously. The gratification for honesty is nonexistant since honorable politicians are shut out, pilloried, smeared, and turned into pariahs. There exists little certainty whether acting less corrupt will provide a greater form of gratification given the seeming impenetrability of establishment politics and the prospect of deterrents—being shut out, pilloried, smeared, and outcast—in exposing corruption or acting honestly. Facing socially-destructive deterrents, hope towards the future dwindles, introducing a feeling of negativity often known as being 'blackpilled'; as one begins to recognize a loss in hope when eying up the prevailing socially-accepted politics establishment monolith.

Earlier in this chapter, I made a reference to how picking a political party resembled a penalty shootout where the goalie has to dive to pick the correct side. Here, the "correct" side is the one promising to overload the national debt even further and to cure the lush's alcoholism by drinking himself sober. The "wrong" side wishes to curb his addiction by effetely telling him the downsides of this condition while uncorking the next bottle of merlot, decantering some single malt, and, when the time is right, cracking open a cold one. The fact remains that it would be career suicide for a politician to correctly diagnose some of the West's ailments— let alone attempt to implement any cures! Pick a side and dive, indeed. Major news outlets will frantically tell you how x politician/ political cause will be apolocalyptic—there's no time, it needs to be thwarted, pronto. The Narrative Complex will weasle narratives into your life trying to convince how there are myriad problems which, only the sagacity, foresight, intellect, benevolence, and will of their chosen political stooges can manage to resolve. They make mountains out of molehills for thorns in their sides, yet memoryhole inconvenient stories which may sully their festering image. Didn't your favorite generic outlet tell you how foreign children are suffering, and how you must throw reason and caution into the wind, open your borders, and ply their extended families with welfare and voting rights? You must become a finely tuned, vocal, and compliant political activist. There's no time to wisely analyse the situation, people are suffering, you know? Once a heartwrenching story has been milked dry, it's time to wheel out the next contrived outrage. An endless source of political energy. Make sure you have a never ending conveyor belt of crying minority children to a populace of self-hating hedonists. And, the point is, there is no time! All of these things need to be resolved now. Now, now, now! Otherwise, you're a racist and a bigot. You're immoral; you're heartless; how can you sleep at night with the knowledge that they're suffering out there—don't you know that Jesus was an immigrant?!

Politics hasn't wrought us nuanced debate, at all. It has needlessly factionalized Western countries for an ideal that never was. The "me-first" mindset rules all. Patience and politeness are for schmucks. There is no time for a pragmatic approach to politics. A politician who can promise resources at the expense of others and hedonistic lifestyles without consequences, while simultaneously denouncing the naysayers is bound to be popular. But, joking aside, there is no time. People need to begin believing again in a future for this vicious, out of control, cycle to be broken. However, implementing a political incentive structure which could promote best and far-sighted behaviors would be mercilessly attacked by all of the Narrative Complex. The way things are, this is too much to request. The current left-right paradigm is purely materialistic—any values which may offer something beyond the material are almost strictly prohibited. The mainstream left traditionally offered generous welfare, protection of industry, and social programs for the betterment of the community, and the mainstream right traditionally sided with small government, private enterprise, and a relatively unhampered market, playing the long game citing how prices will eventually fall once methods in production improve, thus benefiting the more vulnerable members of society. However, both sides have evolved into becoming more materialistic while remaining firmly embedded within the neoliberal rubric. Neither side has little more to offer apart from repackaged neoliberalism: with the right offering small tax cuts and the left offering more welfare and even flirting with the idea of reparations for slavery.

There would need to be a conscientious overhaul in values and collective self-belief to dig the West out of its current rut—something which has been murdered. Nowness must be guilted as selfish. The number of 'somebody-elses' to take responsibility for society's failures, will run out. As the nation is an outdated concept to the PSAP, God doesn't exist to the prevailing socially-accepted politics, and the nuclear family is oppressive; politicians have to find other methods to claim relevance and protect higher values under a valueless prevailing socially-accepted politics. There's been an elevation of the minority as a means to construct values, instill order, and forge loyalty. Offering more social programs as a crutch to support consumption has become a mainstay—it is now a conservative position. Now, in order to protect prevailing socially-accepted politics values, there has to be a repression of the traditional as a crowbar to wedge open unbridled social liberalization, which will inevitably raise social time preferences sky high, stoking up a vicious cycle where gratification becomes the highest—and only—value.

'It's the current year, therefore we must pass X and be tolerant of Y & Z' is the battlecry of somebody with high time preferences, when it comes to politics. It is now a arbitary date in human history, therefore you must accept the policies that I want in order to get a dopamine hit. Politics has become a quasi-religious addiction. And we get the government we deserve, right? For example, populist movements such as Trump and Brexit weren't scripted. And like addicts, they, the establishment, have run themselves into the ground by allowing their political worst nightmares to materialize before their very eyes, through their own high time preferences. They couldn't wait to increase immigration at a more gradual rate. The had to silence dissent because they overplayed their hand. They were called. They were bluffing. The jig is up. Now all forms of wacky politics unfurls itself before us. More progressive pockets of society tolerate the most unthinkably absurd forms of personal expressions. We live in Clown World. Anything goes. They are freefalling down their ideological wormhole. As it transpired, they failed to account for social perception of their ideals because they couldn't wait to make certain taboo or bizarre behaviors more normal due to their high time preferences and low impulse control. They were their own undoing. And the backlash is… colorful—Honk! Honk!

The lines demarcating satire and reality have become blurred. Who would've ever thought an orange billionaire Reality TV star could become president? And this is part of the problem, when it comes to politics. Children, from a young age, are implicitly taught that they have the potential to even become president—if they set their wee mind to it. By convincing the young that they can be whatever they want to be, an environment breeding envy and resentment is fostered as not everyone has the capacity to reach extraordinary goals. For one, low time preferences are needed to becoming a world leader. Fueling resentment often leaves voters feeling as if they're owed something by society as a means to loathe success and to double down on their impulsive lives. It also takes the ability to say "mea culpa" when somebody trips up, for which nobody seems to have the strength. Any politician dwelling outside the orbit of the prevailing socially-accepted politics and the establishment simply cannot screw up as the media would publicly flay them for any indiscretion, no matter how tiny.

Critiquing the prevailing socially-accepted politics in any way as a politician could spell ostracism or sabotage such as in the case of Ron Paul or Bernie Sanders. Stopping to question whether some of the policies or social trends key to the prevailing socially-accepted politics which have blatantly proven disastrous should be put under the microscope. But we don't live in that world. Criticism will be dealt with. And, as a result, the prevailing socially-accepted politics will drift further away from reality, laying the groundwork to its replacement by something in closer harmony with the truth. As the prevailing socially-accepted politics drift further away from reality, it will have to double down on its lunacy like a cornered mongoose. The emperor has no clothes—and more people see it. But giving up power is very difficult to do; doubly so as much has been invested across generations to achieve it. The Narrative Complex is losing its stranglehold on the narrative and reality, slipping into No Man's Land. Politicians are finding it hard to keep up with their incessant scapegoating. Brexit and Trump weren't meant to happen, but they did. Further measures to salvage the narrative must be taken to keep the con alive, which suggests more censorship and harassment of those outside the orbit of the prevailing socially-accepted politics. When the political powder keg ignites, who'll be the poor imbecile to catch that hot potato?

CHAPTER 9

THE DEATH OF GOD

THE GOAL OF THIS CHAPTER is to simply examine the effects of a philosophical death of God and a social outlook on the deferral of gratification. Straight off the bat, with the slow but precipitating death of Christianity in the West, one of the first things that comes to mind is the removal of eternal life. With the removal of eternal life, our time horizons are SIGNIFICANTLY shortened. Imagine, approaching time as if this life were a brief sojourn before eternity, for eternity to be removed from the equation and for this brief sojourn to be all that there is and nothing else. How would people's perception of time be recreated? Perceived time becomes significantly shorter. Life becomes, in a philosophical sense, significantly shorter. With eternal life, collecting material possessions and fleeting experiences seems oddly superfluous on earth if there will be time beyond this life to do so. If this life is all there is then why would I defer gratification beyond my life? Consequences have been removed since there's no final judgement. Why should I behave morally or refrain from taboo acts if there's no sky daddy? I won't be struck down by lightning if I breach any of the ten commandments. Those moralizing

Christians are just lame superstitious goons.

"If God does not exist, everything is permitted"

And that's right: almost anything goes. One of the benefits of a "God-fearing" society is the lack of a need for an all-encompassing, morally policing, state to act as a mediator for all social conflicts. In a society where belief in God trumps belief in the State, social policing at a local level is made possible as most adhere to the same moral code. In a more multicultural and secular society, where individuals and groups adhere to differing, multitudinous, and often conflicting moral codes; the introduction of a large state to mediate and quash discord must, by necessity, arise to return some semblance of order. The divine has been lowered to the human. The greatest manifestation of power on Earth after the philosophically-rebutted God is the state. Politics, in a sense, has filled those large shoes left by God. But it hasn't been enough. To some degree, it has poorly concealed the loss of a joie de vivre manifested in high time preferences when confronting future decisions. Playing the long game when we believed in God was dumb. People are suffering now. Their suffering must be hastily alleviated—now! There exists a particular nowness in a political structure pretending to play the role of God. A willingness to complete, but to complete today as tomorrow may never come. But a belief in a life everlasting requires hope. Much of the presentminded consumerism that comes from 'filling the void' is a product of a loss of hope.

One of the most striking outgrowths of a more secular society has been the collapse in birth rates. Although this phenomenon can be attributed to other factors ranging from wealth creation, advancements in medicine, more hedonistic personal philosophies, the anti-natalist Narrative Complex, etc, a fall in Church attendance rates coincides with a fall in Western birth rates in places such as Ireland. As I have stated in the chapter on The Death of the Family, one of the best things one can do to extend one's time horizons is to have children—a legacy. Even if the parent isn't a believer in organized religion, having children at least extends their stake in the future beyond their own—a life after death, if you may. Without a stake in the future, nowness reigns supreme; an angst to complete as many acts as possible, to fulfill as many possibilities has overtaken sense.

Religiosity tends to be higher in more stressful environments. The West has become relatively destressed, in large part, thanks to the rise in material prosperity. In spite of the rise of material prosperity, stress hasn't fully disappeared—we've merely become better at finding surrogates during the evolution of stress. Wages have stagnated in many countries for decades, while the cost of living soars. The labor market has practically doubled since the political disassembling of the nuclear family in the 60s—not to mention explosive population growth via mass immigration. The stress of Medieval Europe was of a drastically different nature to the stress of today as we no longer have to deal with the open threat of constant war, famine, disease, high infant mortality, etc. Today's stress is of a more material nature—social media, living paycheck to paycheck, the need for

uniqueness/individuation through material enhance-
ments. Stress hasn't fully disappeared. In fact, noticeable
coping mechanisms have become apparent in the rise of
the use of opiates, SSRIs, alcohol, vapid entertainment,
vanity, etc. Instead of there being a need for God to fill
the void, tweaking one's brain chemistry through the
use of drugs, altering one's image, or using addictively
engaging storylines as a refuge for the sheer meaninglessness of modern life has become the norm. The only
identities Westerners are socially allowed to hold are
either atomized faceless NPC producing-consumer or
self-hating prevailing socially-accepted political activist
who gleefully throws away their society for headpats
from minorities. Either way, on the question of time,
there's little reason to look beyond the tip of one's nose
in long-term decision making.

Out of the philosophical death of God, we've seen
the emergence of several personal philosophies from
nihilism, absurdism, egoism, communism, socialism,
anarchism, etc, which have sought to replace and fulfill
the role of a transcendental being, but to no avail. Most
of these philosophies are both materialist and universalist. The two political philosophies aforementioned which
have partly acted as a replacement to the monotheistic
God—communism and socialism—proved catastrophic
genocidal failures in the 20th century. There are many
arguments as to why they failed including economic
issues, poor governance, attempting to implement a
political philosophy which is at odds with human
nature, external influences, etc. However, the most
striking failure—aside from the millions brutally slain—

of the USSR has been the surprising recrudescence of Orthodox faith in a post-Soviet Russia. After three generations of state-mandated antitheism—a whole "living memory"—Russians are flocking back to the church in droves.

Today, without a shadow of a doubt, the dominant political philosophy is neoliberalism. Universalist, globalist, materialist, and intolerably anti-theist in nature—only for Christians, of course—neoliberalism is the faith of the establishment and its cronies. Progressivism, although wishing to distance itself from neoliberalism, has become an unsuspecting victim to be absorbed by neoliberalism. The free market predilection of mainstream conservative fits in nicely with the capitalist tendencies of neoliberalism, although the defenseless so-called conservative "values" are broadly rejected by the gatekeepers of this modern secular faith. Progressivism is merely neoliberalism's protestantism. Conservatism, while still somewhat liberal, is the equivalent to Arianism—to be denounced by the neoliberal consensus for its stance on hot topics. Conservatives are racist, homophobic, and any other meaningless buzzword to simply denote 'heretical'. Mainstream conservatism is merely a defunct branch of liberalism.

Unrepentantly anti-nationalist, anti-racist, anti-bigotry, anti any unprogressive -ism, in fact, neoliberalism is our future and the end of history, whether we like it or not. Superficially, this elitist philosophy which only serves to enrich a class of 21st century robber-barons who sell their nations for lucre, promises to eradicate all forms of bigotry, bring diverse peoples closer, authoritatively dismantle authoritarianism, and end all wars; ineluctably dragging us closer to a world unencumbered by borders, ethnic feuds, and local governments. Capital has got places to be—we can't let troglodytic antiquities such as borders act as impediments.

Don't you know that through their sage creative destruction, deindustrialisation, removal of tariffs, and offshoring, you'll all be $15 a month richer in 5 years time? It's worth it, n'est pas? Neoliberals are basically little more than our red-flaging-waving chums from the last century—they just are married to or marred by such rigid anti-capitalist dogmas. By using the free-market as a carrot on a stick to the center and the right, they present themselves as more palatable to the petit bourgeoisie. Without trying to ignite class consciousness, neoliberals, in part, have managed to fulfill many planks set out in The Communist Manifesto.

Moreover, the multinational neoliberal social credo rests on the far-left to both extend and appease their consumer base—Millennials, Gen Z, and the up-and-coming. We've seen major corporations—often chaotically—virtue signal to progressive causes such as LGBT+. Among younger generations, holding homophobic views is a no-no. In city areas, which also tend to be more consumeristic, any progressive transgression can amount to social ostracism. But, a more consumerist society, almost by necessity, needs to have high time preferences; it needs to be wanting to consume, to fill a void. For big corporations, a society which chooses to exercise caution with their finances, to defer gratification, would prove deleterious to their revenue. In order for large companies to reap large profits, there needs to be an extensive consumer base ready to cough up their bucks at a moment's notice whever the latest enhanced product hits the shelves. A godless society is a hedonistic society, or, at least, has a hedonistic streak. You would be judged for your actions by an omniscient being. Fetters on our carnal instincts had been applied by our sky-daddy for centuries. Now that they've been removed, let's screw, debauch, and consume till we drop. There will be no consequences for our actions.

And, not only that, we will have commercials tacitly cheering us on from the sidelines. There is no father figure condemning us from up above. There is no father figure condemning us from home either. Life is short. Youth is shorter. Youth must be preserved and harnessed for the longest time. For women, in particular, this involves indulging in the hollowest forms of vanity—to desperately cling onto one's looks and withering sexual market value for as long as possible. For men, it's to sow their oats to the aforementioned women. Screw, debauch, consume: believing in a God that may or may not exist is silly—what if you're wrong; what if you spent your short life praising and following a social construct erected to oppress the masses? You could've spent your time seeking all forms of forbidden pleasures instead.

In Western countries, the few remaining Christian traditions that are celebrated have become grostequely commercialized. You can celebrate Christmas, not for its traditions, but for its timely opportunity to sell goods.

Likewise for Easter. (Yes, yes, I know they were originally pagan holidays. Let's move on.) For Christmas, there
have been stories in the media informing us how carols
with "Jesus Christ" have been removed to avoid causing
offense, Santa—who isn't part of the original story, but
has become an inseparable mainstay to Christmas
time—has now come out of the closet: he's in an interra-
cial homosexual relationship. Why not? It's the current
year, after all. If you were to watch UK Christmas
advertisements on TV, you'll see families who, let's say,
had no ancestors who fought in the Battle of the Somme,
and portray a thoroughly un-British Christmas to score
woke Brownie points. Easter has also been relegated to a
consumerist abomination. Easter eggs, to avoid causing
offense to minorities, have been renamed in certain
supermarkets. I guess you can celebrate Christian
traditions, but only the ones where big business can
make a buck or two. Just remember to not celebrate the
traditions wholeheartedly. In fact, just buy stuff instead
and send people a "season's greetings" card; that way,
you'll avoid offending your peers.

With the philosophical death of God, materialist philosophies come into the forefront as a replacement. It is
my observation that, for most adherents of these
philosophies, their philosophy isn't enough to plaster
over the void in their lives—a craving for something
greater than oneself. In the absence of God, people have
attempted to use "The State", humanity, themselves, and
other constructs at their disposal to span the void. But
still, the perception of time remains stunted. Gratification must come within one's lifetime without an

extension of life; either via a belief in everlasting life or by having children. Consumption is a great way of filling the void—temporarily. Your material—and spiritual—needs are satiated in the here and now. But what about the future? We'll cross that bridge when we get to it. Have you got enough funds/savings in order to scratch the consumerist itch? Don't worry, you can put that on your credit card. Why wait? You can chase the consumerist dragon.

The fundamental problem with materialist philosophies is that they tend to be materialistic in practice too. A high proportion of atheists and anti-theists tend to be on the left, politically. An impure distillation of leftist views would be to say that an enlargement of the state/government is their main course of action. Most people on the left would be self-described "progressives", liberals, social democrats, and democratic socialists. Fewer would be found on the communist, socialist, anarchist, or one of the fifty shades of red on the fringes. The main body of the left gravitates around the "progressive" banner. Progressivism is, undoubtedly, a form of secular religiosity as there are cults of personality (as there are to the right but to a lesser degree); there are forms of heresies—racism, bigotry, sexism, any other -ism; a progressive is more likely to cut somebody out of their life for having the wrong politics; there are demonic villains within competing political faiths—Trump, Farage, Bannon, Coulter, et al. What's more, for many, abandoning progressivism will spell nihilism. Progressivism for many is a bulwark to crushing nihilism. The atheist progressive simply cannot return to organized religion especially after anathema-tizing it for most of intellectual life. They have cornered themselves within their progressive faith; which is what endows them a near fundamentalist fanaticism when their political beliefs are interrogated. In renouncing one's faith in the cathedral of progress, many-a time they are committing social seppuku. Living in coastal progressive strongholds and having the wrong political views will spell hermitage for most. Moreover, progress hitches a ride by amplifying many canons of Critical Theory which serves to deconstruct every aspect of Western life. And Critical Theory serves only to decon-struct—not to replace, creating a soulsucking vacuum, without giving a moment's thought to consider what may come by tearing down values, customs, and traditions painfully preserved across several generations and failing to offer a viable replacement.

In Western and Northern Europe, Islam poses an existential threat to the progressive order. Islam is underpinned by a belief in the divine whereas progres-sivism in self-deification. To sustain a progressive order with maximum social freedom, it has to be agreed by every extant member of the collectively progressive society; otherwise, it will splinter and balkanize as it's ultimate values are wafer thin. Progressivism also allies itself with Islam, viewing it as an oppressed group, but Islam will eviscerate progressivism once reaching a critical mass, kicking off something similar to another Iranian Revolution. Individuals won't lay down their lives to defend progress—they value themselves and their uninhibited present gratification made possible by progressive values over progressivism in itself. There's a bizarre phenomenon where some progressive individuals who cozy up to Islam take the plunge and convert to the faith, abandoning their previously secularist outlook. Islam provides more meaning than an ideology whose raison d'etre is the critique and deconstruction of Western traditions. Western traditions are now off limits, but Islam offers something greater to the neophyte than deconstructed and 'racist' Western traditions. Islam offers order for the relativistic chaos of what is presented as progress.

The Confession of one's sins urges religious individuals to become cognizant of the actions and to experience guilt. Confession compels somebody to reel off what they have done wrong in the scope of their faith. Being wary of one's sins enables them to identify that there maybe future consequences and to avoid acting socially undesirably. You will be brought forth before your maker, judged, and condemned for the rest of eternity—and that's a lot of time. This type of message won't resonate with many youngsters. Many youngsters have been deprived of any moral authority for much of their lives. But it is clear that society, in spite of the tremendous progress made in wealth, technology, and science; hasn't been able to cover all bases. In America, there's an awful suicide and opioid crisis. Suicide is the ultimate expression of nihilism: where life becomes so unbearable, you fail to care about the consequences to be suffered by your loved ones—your loved ones' wellbeing ceases to outrank the pain of existence. Suicide—with the exception of martyrdom—is the worst sin to commit. Life, being the highest gift to receive, has commanded itself the power to self-destruct. Life, ideally, shouldn't desire its own negation. But there exists a rampant lack of respect for life, an irreverent ingratitude. If life is pure suffering, time, in the future, cannot be dominated to find meaning or gratification. The disrepect for life has manifested itself in political movements. Abortion, the termination of a fetus, is now being extended into the third trimester in some places.

Some political activists are toying with the idea of infanticide. But oftentimes the reasons offered for abortion or infanticide is to protect the very murdered child or the mother's interests. If a person is incapable of raising a child, they shouldn't be engaging in unprotected sex with unloyal or unstable providers. Society shouldn't be burdened with the financial and social costs of their indiscretions. The willfulness to engage in such practices indicates a profound lack of self-respect, low impulse control, a lack of judgement, high time preferences, and selfishness—for both consenting parties. Bringing a child into the world requires a great deal of responsibility. They are the tomorrow.

Although superficially admirable, promoting an unrestrained live-and-let-live social philosophy without consequence generates an incentive structure where people live for each departing moment. Why care about the future if the government will take care of my missteps? There are few nasty financial and social consequences if I screw up. I can't be excluded, I can't be discriminated against—unless I'm a white male... eww—people must be understanding, people have to accept my errors—which were somebody else's fault, anyway—and so on and so forth. How can you be a Christian when they launched Crusades, had corrupt Popes, schisms, pedo priests, etc? How could anybody believe in a skyghost when this scientific theory inches us closer to the real, scientifically-proven, first origins story. God creating the world in six days then resting on the seventh? Hogwash! Religion, provided it's Christian, is under constant attack. Other, more socially primitive religions are given a free pass to ensure that cultural sensitivities aren't flared. We're creating a lovely multicultural social tapestry by failing to scrutinize other religious customs as the needle would prick the spinster. Christianity has been defanged since the Reformation and ain't got no real bite. Some denominations of Christianity have fallen into the trap of attracting support by cheapening the original message by allowing concessions for social progress. This has proven disastrous as older members are alienated and hip, young, new potential neophytes' intelligence supercedes the need for a busybody skydaddy to make them feel guilty for fornicating and disrespecting their parent(s). Also, how could they join an institution loudly proclaimed heretical by the progressive cathedral? Many young adults have latched onto the logos of progressive cathedral. Life ends with themselves as the highest being. Why would their perception of time reach beyond their own life? Why would gratification be deferred for a higher purpose if they themselves are that higher purpose? There is no meaning in low time preferences when they are the highest value. Some say that humanity is the greatest end. Realistically, how many could authentically love those unrelated to them more than themselves? Even then, we could count the amount of great individuals who dedicated their lives to the service to humanity in its entirety on our fingers; but we could never count the number of individuals who dedicated their lives to their God, nation, and family as they would be impossible to number.

FOOTNOTE: *I am merely an illustration for the perception of time horizons when individuals value intangible values as greater than themselves.*

CHAPTER 10

THE BOOMERS

I MENTIONED IN THE LAST CHAPTER the great responsibility of bringing children into the world. Baby boomers are often used as a scapegoat for many of America's social problems in certain political circles. Boomers are seemingly afflicted by an inability and indifference towards understanding many concerns of the younger generations. However, I won't give Boomers all the blame. Boomers were raised at the zeitgeist of American exceptionalism. A wholesome image of white picket fences, sharply dressed handsome men, well-groomed feminine women, happy children, and hope for the future. Boomers were raised with very little hardship and ample opportunity. Many alive today are homesick for a period which wasn't their own. They longingly gaze back in time where many of today's problems back then would've been thought inconceivable. Economically speaking, however, there was much cheap credit fueling (push factors) a prosperous job market, raising time preferences. A blue-collar worker could support a large family as sole bread-winner. Things were looking good, until they weren't.

As a whole, the boomer generation lived a very sheltered life. Broken homes were few and far between compared to today. Long term unemployment was alien to many. People could walk the street at night without fear of assault. Neighborhoods could leave their front doors unlocked. Communities were safe. But they took what they had for granted. During the 50s and 60s we saw the gestation period of the modern Narrative Complex, which announced its bilious birth with the rise of the civil rights movements, the 1965 Immigration act, and the Peace Movement. On the right-wing of politics, American patriotism was corrupted by Trotskyite entryists in Neoconservatism, using right-wing patriotism as the emotional standard bearer to endless foreign policy. The left-wing was on the ascendency as America had laid the foundations to its collapse. The left could present themselves as the panacea to socio-political ills: the Peace Movement against the Vietnam War, Women's and sexual liberation from the authoritarian personality of the American nuclear family, psychoactives and free love acted as the dambusters for social repression, opening a Pandora's Box of social horrors beautifully captured by today's Clown World meme. The Frankfurt School slowly relocated itself to America where it could spread its ideas, digging its claws into academia, trickling into the media and Entertainment Industry. Ideas completely contradictory to American ideals were handed an opportunity to metastasize and spread, leaving behind a terminally ill social experiment.

The most spoilt generation in human history revolted against its own spoilt self. It was the harbinger of its own demise, but since they binned responsibility—in the form of myriad social programs, socializing the costs of their high time preferences on the succeeding generation—they have ushered in the Last Days of Rome for the American experiment. Under their stewardship, we've witnessed an unprecedented deepening of the American National Debt, the astronomical Debt/GDP ratio, the malignant cancerous growth of the state, the erasure of Western values, the demise of the nuclear family, the introduction of multiple dependence-provoking social programs, the demographic displacement of their generation's children, the unrecognizable transformation of multiple big cities, soaring crime rates, racial hatred, collapsing church attendance rates, etc—but at least they got theirs, right? They got to enjoy their orgiastic narcotic pleasures at the expense of their children which they didn't even consider. Digging heads into the ground and tilting at windmills to deflect feeling guilt from their patent lack of care and responsibility. Of course, the Narrative Complex was the ideological fountainhead to this massive—and rapid—shift in consciousness. Instead of unshackling themselves from the repressive authoritarian personalities of their parents, they've shackled their children, prying their eyes open to watch how their civilization burns before them. The guilt must be too hard to bear. Pathetically misapplying exhausted tenets to cover for their errors is a favored course of action. America's change was seismic. Europe's change was seismic, too. If you were to show footage of the modern Western world today to people in the 1950s, how would they react? How many would think of it as an improvement. We have all the Ivy League metrics to prove how things have never been better—materially. But is this really the case? The future was forgotten. They got stuck living in the vanishing present as if the future would never come.

The Boomer generation is a real-life case study for when a society lives with collectively high time preferences. They turn their backs on all the boring traditions as a mild impediment to their instant gratification. A loss in belief of those traditions is passed down to their children and their children's children. Eventually, new values need to be discovered in the absence of former values. But none of the new values need preserving since they constantly shift. How can you have low time preferences if what you know and cherish constantly changes? It becomes impossible to act or create a moral framework whose time horizons exceed the length of one's nose. Even children, in the modernized economy where women have become men's competitors, have been brought up by others—daycare, TV, school—since their parents are off working a lot of the time. They aren't around to instill the best values; that is, of course, if those values are still believed in. They entrusted others—whose interests weren't allied to their children's—to raise them instead of taking responsibility while they chased more materialistic ends, using trendy buzzwords as empty excuses for their lack of care. They got their reward. They had their fun. They were off having fun when they should've been vigilant. Fun was exploited as a distraction, as a method to destroy. They had all the necessary pull factors to induce them to live irresponsibly.

And the few stoic enough to resist temptation from that generation are stuck to assume responsibility for the consequences of their contemporaries. The reality is that the Boomer generation has irreparably altered America—for the worse. They chose fun over duty. Living for today instead of tomorrow. They have the puerile audacity to attempt to justify or ignore their social legacy. In the long run, they're all dead—and it's their children's children who are stuck, footing the bill. Their parents may have done them a mild disservice in spoiling them. The threat of global communism, despite the euphoria after defeating the Nazis, loomed large. After surviving yet another great war which killed off European Imperialism, it was time for the American Eagle to soar to the stratosphere and become the big dog in global foreign policy. America could proudly flex their pecs as the bastion of freedom and burgeoning global policeman. Back at home, business thrived with cheap credit. Their childhoods may have been more pampered, but the rise of the entertainment industry's prominence, mass advertising, and the proliferation of new ideas via the Narrative Complex hurriedly changed social consciousness. Nationalism became increasingly taboo after the Second World War. The jingoistic gung-ho attitude to the Vietnam War served to dent nationalist sentiment. The progressive, social-experimental ideas which irrupted during the 60s derisively challenged preexisting Christian ethics; which consequently dealt a fatal blow to the sacredness of the nuclear family.

All values higher than oneself—faith, nation, family—had been irreparably damaged. All that now reigned supreme was the individual and its immediate gratification. Nothing else matters. Nothing of import was preserved. The introduction of the Great Society by LBJ presented push factors to higher time preferences as will as a corresponding meteoric rise to single motherhood rates, indicating the agonizing death of the nuclear family structure. The devil may care attitude to fun marked by the 60s necessitated the removal of God; thus signifying the removal of consequences. And the 1965 Immigration Act marked the beginning of the end of the nation. What received values do the post-Boomer generations have to live for—apart from the continuance of life to no higher purpose? The Boomer generation, with their high-time preferences, deserted vigilance in order to consume, screw, and enjoy. And now, if a younger generation complains about disposable income or the job market wearing thing—in part due to the impulsive policies ushered in since the early 60s—the member of the younger generations are dispassionately commanded to simply find a job. And while Boomers have a point when criticizing the weak-willed younger generation, the question begs: who raised them? Because the generation of the various social revolutions had it so good, they abandoned responsibility and socialized consequence. High time preferences and the possibility to offset the come down from the good times means the younger generations will get to suffer the hangover for just a fraction of the partying.

CHAPTER 11

CHAOS

LONGER TERM INVESTMENTS TEND to be deemed as carrying a greater risk factor than shorter investments due to the greater length of time in which the possibility for unforeseen events altering information, demand, values, etc, to arise. Likewise, when it comes to an individual perception of time, when information constantly changes, technological creative destruction dictates demands, manufactured media outrages, Narrative Complex' narratives flow on, and other similar events occur on such a regular basis; how are values constructed? Amid moral, linguistic, cultural, and other forms of relativism which have become an immutable mainstay in Western societies, how is long-term planning facilitated when truth itself becomes undervalued due to its fragile nature under current social trends. Furthermore, many publications have hailed the dawn of the post-truth era. People are encouraged to follow their feelings—feelings which have been conditioned by the narratives spun by the Narrative Complex to further the establishment's agendas. Objective truth is out the window and technology moves at a stellar pace, living beyond today could, in many cases, seem both futile and ludicrous. There's no guarantee that what I know and cherish now will remain down the line. Better keep those options open. How can you allow yourself to be pinned down by one choice. Choice in this case is an affliction. One is surrounded by choice, subjective truth, and all forms of relativism. Where does one cast their anchor? Time's importance is reduced when under siege by a distortion of truth. Time can sit on the backburner as tomorrow the information can change again—you wouldn't wanna be left behind. In more unstable societies, there's a tendancy to live fast and die young. And although we enjoy an incredible level of comfort and wealth in Western societies; it seemingly takes the edge off much of the instability as a distraction.

One doesn't notice the relentless change around us in what we know, what's trendy, what's socially acceptable/unacceptable, who to love, who to hate, as we're plugged into technology or activities which distract us from the bigger picture. Chaos in the form of a 'live and let live' mentality, ensures a 'living for today' mentality since the only thing guaranteed in the future is change. Values are untethered as truth is merely subjective—and subject to whimsical emotions. Low time preferences amid chaos requires the discovery of values based on enduring truths. If everything were to be subjective, then deferring gratification would be somewhat irrational as one's perception of gratification may change throughout the course of time. However, realizing the irrationality of deferring gratification under such unstable conditions would be to recognize reason as an enduring value in itself. The extreme ontological inauthenticity of modern instability compounded by the fallacious narratives churned out by the Narrative Complex sets in motion a self-destructive vicious cycle glorified as trendy or empowering by adherents of the prevailing socially-accepted politics. For low time preferences to become desirable, the pay off from deferring gratification into the future must be realizable to some degree. One must be able to somewhat conceptualize how they are to be rewarded for their foresight. Today's chaotic, epistemologically unstable, and ontologically inauthentic lifestyle simply adds more factors to be taken into consideration when acting long term; thus making any conceptualization of future gain a tougher calculation to make. On the whole, even the more future-oriented individuals may have to raise their time preferences to adjust for constant change in the forms of technological growth, scientific advancements, political upheavals, etc.

CHAPTER 12

THE DEATH OF DISCIPLINE

OUT OF ALL THE RECENT quasi-fringe civil rights movements including "acne rights", transspeciesism, transableism, etc, the one which really encapsulates the West's dearth and death of discipline has been "fat acceptance". Within this quasi-movement, we've seen activists claim that dieting is a capitalist sleight of hand, how obesity is just as healthy as somebody within the normal weight range, or how a certain activist got "triggered" by a cancer charity's advertisement which linked obesity to cancer. Immediately, a denial of reality can be identified within this movement. Of course, when it comes to obesity, more than just overeating needs to be addressed as there could be underlying psychological issues which compels the individual to overeat. Eating also yields a feeling of satisfaction and can be used to fill a void in one's life. When it comes to Fat Acceptance, it's not solely the obese individuals who piercingly shriek for society to accept and make concessions for their abnormal size, but those who go along with the charade. Weight loss is hard. It requires discipline—discipline which people simply don't have. In our opulent, plentiful, wealthy Western world, struggling over providing enough food for all as almost been relegated to the history books. Anybody can cheaply acquire junk food—it's omnipresent. If the stigma surrounding overeating is removed, other people have to deal with the consequences in the form of cost. This form of ill-discipline is continuous.

Staying at a healthy weight—for most—requires constant vigilance of what one eats. Sliding off the rails is all to easy, especially when one's imperfections and indiscretions are lauded. Obesity puts extreme pressure on healthcare services; plus, many of the Fat Activists tend to be nestled on the left, which calls for universal healthcare. Now, we have a situation where some people what to eat, balloon up to an unhealthy size, call it normal, demand for companies and the state alike to bend over backwards to facilitate their lifestyle, suggest that they are just as attractive as svelte, trim, and nubile women, and, when their lifestyle catches up with them, you're the one who has to pay for their healthcare. Don't like it? Well, you're the bigot.

But where has this all come from? Being oppressed or having a disability is a form of milking power. Society has supposedly wronged these individuals for so long, it's time to redress the balance. The way things are going, power isn't granted to the just, deserving, meritorious; but to the "oppressed", the mediocre, the ill-disciplined, the loud, the needy—almost a complete inversion. A so-called "Fat Activist", under any other circumstances, wouldn't have much to offer anybody, let alone command such referential power. The only discipline necessitated by their role is to be consistently in a caloric surplus. Power should be parcelled out by one's achievements, persistence, will, expertise, foresight, temperance, stoicism; and not by their ability to put down those expressing their concern with their habit. In order to gain power—not just power derived from the state—time needs to be factored into the equation. A goal needs to be set out. Obstacles will inevitably creep in. Working hard for an inestimable length of time to, sometimes, not even see any concrete results is a sacrifice which needs to be made. Having a purpose greater than oneself is a terrific motivator—such as a God, family, or nation.

I have taken "Fat Acceptance" as my example to illustrate the correlation between a "praiseworthy" lack of discipline and time preference. Dieting can be painful—you're lightheaded, moody, bereft of energy, tired, hungry, tempted, etc. Sometimes, it can be too difficult to go alone, and you require external help—help reminding you of your goal. Unfortunately, when others are accepting of that ill-discipline, they won't wholeheartedly support the cause and spill cliched platitudes such as "you do you, boo", "I think you're great just the way you are", "Whatever makes you feel good." Sadly, it's way easier and less time-consuming to regurgitate a cliche then pound a quarter-pounder than to make somebody sad by reminding them of their condition, the fact that their condition has to be addressed, and the unknown amount of time—then maintenance—to resolve their condition. Discipline is pain. Discipline is wholly unglamorous—the Narrative Complex demonizes discipline. Discipline requires sacrifice. And, most dauntingly, discipline needs repetition.

Repetition to do the same painful task when you'd rather be doing something else is made easier when there's a purpose in mind. If the predominating incentive structure frowns upon discipline (toxic masculinity) or the purpose of said discipline, then why would one go about improving oneself? It would be, frankly, pointless. But now, the incentive structures we have in place repudiate discipline, revile discipline, chastise discipline—and all forms of discipline. All forms of crutches are readily available in case one slips up, both physical and verbal. Articles complain about gym bros being right-wing assholes, right wing politics and aversion to body odor, presentation, hair, etc, all being party to a line of political thinking. Bearing in mind that the term "right-wing" is something of a pejorative—something akin to uttering "Voldemort" in Harry Potter.

For our societal lack of discipline, Game Theory comes in handy to illustrate the social pay offs for engaging in a task which requires discipline outside of one's labor:

Example:

Fat Acceptance Activist to lose 140lbs to become healthy weight:

Scenario 1: continue to pile on pounds, continue to have social media following and donations, not have to exert oneself and lose social media status,

Scenario 2: Take unknowable length of time, lose original social media following, eat foods which derive no pleasure, undergo rigorous exercise program, lose weight, extend life expectancy, improve fertility and sexual attractiveness,

Both of these scenarios involve a question of individual subjective value and how each pay off can be perceived. If one's thinking is formed in such a way, the easy option which doesn't require a low time preference can look more appetizing and have a greater Net Present Value or payoff to the individual.

Discipline, although repetitious, holds an element of uncertainty. Uncertainty can be something undesirable, especially if one's values change throughout the course of undergoing a weightloss transformation. But, to a certain degree, life itself is uncertain, and the future pay offs which require generous helpings of discipline need to exceed the hardship to be suffered in the meantime. In order for us to enjoy the current incentive structure where pain, sacrifice, and discipline are on their way to become relics of the past; somebody else must've sweat bullets and toiled blood in order to provide these luxuries. To remind ourselves of our humanity, we (in Western middle class society) must now go out of our way to experience hardship. The incentive structure in place is gratification and no deferral, responsibility, sacrifice, or consequence. And without knowing the value of deferral, our unleashed will-to-gratification will surely exceed the limitations of production, eventually.

CHAPTER 13

ECONOMICS

WE LIVE IN AN ECONOMY. Sorry for the tacky joke.

To the shamans of neoliberalism, a steady 3% growth is paramount to appeasing the wraths of the GDP Gods. Western countries have become hollow, cultureless economic zones; representing a decadent and atavistic society whose multiple ethnic groups only present themselves as an inconvenience to market forces. What we have is presented as free trade, but this is very disingenuous considering the voluminous regulations, special interest groups, lobbyists, subsidies, preferential tax rates, and other "unmarketlike" conditions distorting the price system and competition. There is, I must stress, more to life than homo oeconomicus, economics, and accumulating material wealth; but the less "woke" substratum of the Narrative Complex uses shapeless and marginal jumps in material wealth as motivators to promote mass immigration—leading to the cultural dilution of nations, thus opening them to bastardized forms of "free trade". Mass immigration simultaneously depresses wage levels while increasing government spending and housing prices, creating a pernicious illusion of economic productivity. The cult of GDP cries for more immigrations. The constant growth looks fantastic on paper—fantastic! But, what is the cost of it all? Western national debts have soared like the American Eagle; social programs are woefully underfunded; public spending has skyrocketed to cover the disproportionately higher rates of crime, single motherhood, unemployment, schooling, policing, etc, from third world mass immigration; healthcare services are insolvent; housing is inadequate; and the list goes on. But, on paper, this represents economic productivity despite nothing of value being created. Our debt-based economies need constant influxes of new workers to keep the con alive. Our state pensions can only be kept afloat by bringing in the children … I mean, workers, our preceding generations chose not to have. Without constant growth, we'd have recession—a recession that would make The Great Depression look like a cakewalk—leading to deflation, less tax revenue, and mass unemployment. The emperor's naked backside will finally be revealed for all. This frail economic house of cards will be faced by the prospect of a hurricane, but no politician wants to be the poor schmuck who catches this hot potato. Winning elections in the here and now, failed attempts at social engineering, and a reprehensible indifference towards the future—all under the stewardship of corrupt, self-serving politicians—has landed us in this pickle. They're dead and buried, while we're buried under unassailable levels of debt we didn't accrue.

Originally, the idea of time preference hails from The Austrian School of economics. In a pure market economy—free from all government interference—interest rates, being a price, would be determined by time preferences. In such an economy, money would be sound or at least backed by something to retain its value—such as gold—and currency debasement at the hands of issuers of money would be minimized by pressures—such as bankruptcy, loss of reputation, bank runs, etc. Therefore, a financial system in this abstract market economy would (or should) be 100% backed by specie. When financial institutions have a larger supply of specie (gold, silver, precious stones, etc), this would indicate that consumers are more geared towards saving, suggesting a LOW time preference. Conversely, when financial institutions have a smaller supply of specie to loan out, this would indicate that consumers are more geared towards consuming, suggesting a HIGH time preference. Now, as I have mentioned, interest rates in a pure market economy would be a price (in the true sense of the word as interest rates are tampered with by central banks—a form of price control) reflecting the laws of supply and demand. As specie could be converted and reused as credit, more specie signifies more supply of credit thus reducing interest rates (price). Conversely, less specie signifies less supply of credit thus increasing interest rates. Furthermore, when interest rates are low—suggesting a low aggregate time preference—long-term investments, requiring a low time preference as gratification is further away, become more attractive and available. Vice versa, high interest rates indicate less specie suggesting a high aggregate time preference and a market more disposed towards immediate consumption than saving/investing/building.

Price As Information

Prices are an invaluable universal language. Prices and the price system communicate to us crucial information regarding the allocation of commodities, time, labor, etc. An economy without a price system cannot yield a society greater than a rudimentary, splintered, and decentralized agricultural arrangement. Resource allocation without a price system is impossible as a central authority cannot gather the necessary information. In a situation where both economic—prices, money supply, interest rates, tax rates—and social information—language, norms, politics, immigration—are in an accelerated rate of change, perceived future pay-offs are distorted given the greater risks in the changeability and additon of variable factors, making long-term economic and social decision-making even trickier. Time preferences, in order to be kept low, must require information or perceived objective truth to be relatively stable. Prices convey information; therefore, one, while making long term decisions with their finances, would hope that prices remain relatively stable in the time period between the manifestation of a desire and its eventual gratification.

Opportunity Cost & Value Scales

As I've said before, a concept in the future doesn't exist

in the present. Although calculations can be made to determine whether that concept or project is worthwhile, until its fully realized; unforeseen risks, obstacles, issues, and other curve balls can be lobbed in the meantime making the concept/project less attractive. It must be noted that our current economic order, neoliberalism, unites the worst elements of both worlds acting like a ventilator to prevent its own very system from flatlining. Neoliberalism has incorporated the selfish consumerism of capitalism and the presentminded parasitism of socialism. And the unhappy marriage of these two elements are its lifeblood. In a democratic order, neoliberalism pacifies both sides of the economic aisle: on the left, ample welfare and social assistance; on the right, free markets. By instilling passivity on both mainstream political wings, it creates a certain consumerist trance-like peace. Have many people asked why major corporations vocally support far-left social positions? Major corporations also advocate for higher minimum wages—pour quoi? A higher minimum wage would make life a lot more difficult for smaller competitors and give the same major corporations a reason to begin automating redundant job positions. Even if unemployment were to rise, the unemployed would receive social assistance in the form of welfare, and they'd still wish to consume. Neoliberalism is meant to resemble mostly free market principles with state intervention to finely tune its performance. The market economy is consumer driven—and this is important to remember. If the consumer base is presentminded, with a will-to-gratify, the profit margins of large corporations would be enormous.

However, if that consumer base were to be less materialistic and/or religious, with low time preferences and their goals distantly future-oriented; the ability of large corporations to reap enormous profits would be massively stunted. Information—the narrative—must change to reflect the profit-motive of large corporations. Information is to shepherd individuals into a materialistic state of presentmindedness so that they wish to consume to give their lives the remotest meaning instead of more tradition methods of adding value to their lives. With advertisements, entertainment narratives, trendy hedonist philosophies all grooming our desires to consume, even the most fervent anti-capitalists can be seen typing into their $1000 laptop, donning the latest designer clothing, and sipping a Starbucks low-fat soy latte. Everything has been commoditized as a method to decode information to be transformed into identifiable desires in a corporatized world that has embargoed higher meaning.

The Individual

Don't ask questions
Just consume product
Then get excited
For next Products

The incentive structures at play in looking at our economic situation are similar to the time preferences of famished piranhas when a calf with a broken leg falls off the river bank. Consume, consume, consume—and consume some more. Push and pull factors both play a role in this frenzied form of consumerism. Moreover, many individuals saddle themselves with high levels of debt in the form of tuition which they often spend a good chunk of their life paying off. Long term financial planning is discouraged and disposable income is reduced by the existence of these debts, which, more often than not, are for worthless degrees that have nothing to do with the individual's chosen career path. With less disposable income, more debts accrue in the meantime, making saving a more challenging feat. Debt culture has become pervasive in tandem with the growing materialism in Western society. If you want to compete with the brightest and best in Ivy League Schools, well, you've gotta put yourself into a few starting-annual-salaries-worth of debt before ever securing employment. Not only will you receive a thorough education steeped in the prevailing socially-accepted politics' values, but you'll also have a chunk of your wage scythed away every month for the first half of your career. Neat, huh?

The assumption of debt is almost a perverse form of giving meaning to one's life in a nihilistic economo-centric neoliberal order as monthly repayments become a carrot on a stick, a raison d'etre for homo oeconomicus whose plenteous desires have become affordably commoditized. It doesn't end there though. Corporations are merely pull factors in raising social time preferences as they tempt or pull consumers in with their siren song of colorful, psychologically stimulating advertisements and product placement. The modern

State's role over monetary and fiscal policies can push consumers into presentminded consumerism to beef up yearly economic figures. Therefore, the individual is sandwiched between two factors leading them to the same consumerist pastures.

A market-based economy is a consumer-driven economy. Corporations supposedly cater to the demands of consumers. But what if we can put the horse behind the cart? What if corporations—whose existence in their current forms unequivocally need consumers with high time preferences to keep afloat—can dictate consumer demands? On the one hand, through advertisment and product placement—which often hitches a ride on the entertainment industry—corporations can peak consumer interests, and, on the other, through the very narratives promoted by the entertainment industry, shape consumer's thoughts to become willing to purchase goods they could never otherwise live without. The Narrative Complex becomes mutually beneficial to megacorporations. A society whose values are more grounded in the transcendental will have both lower time preferences and a weaker desire to be a slave to their consumerist passions.

Push

The American Dollar and Pound Sterling, for example, have both lost upwards of 95% of their value in the past hundred years. Unless you have hard assets or millions tied up in investments, your money, your disposable income is being siphoned away in a contemptuous form of stealth tax which economists laud as a method to stimulate the economy when it stagnates—inflation. And it does exactly what it says on the tin: stimulates consumption. However, it's no economic wizardry; inflation burns a hole in your pocket by decreasing the real value of the lint-covered change in your pocket, and, increasing prices encourage you to spend in favor of saving as inflation reduces purchasing power. Those with hard assets are saved from inflation to a certain degree as their assets retain value vis-a-vis inflation. Those living from paycheck-to-paycheck to those who have little present need for hard assets—cars, homes, precious metal, (investments of sorts), etc—see their income, disposable income, slowly evaporate like a pond in late summer. Saving becomes less desirable, creating an incentive structure which punishes thrift and rewards present consumption as their ever-devalued money is exchanged for commodities which holds onto its value.

Controversially, some of the superficial economic effects of mass immigration include increased demand for housing driving up prices, and increased supply of low to unskilled labor driving down wages—a very unhappy combo of a higher cost of living and less income. Establishment economists will glibly dismiss these claims with graphs mendaciously drawn up to promote whatever agenda the establishment wishes to promote. Women's liberation and the decline of the nuclear family has also mimicked the economic pressures of mass immigration—increase demand for housing, increase supply of labor. In the case of women's liberation and the decline of the nuclear family, although some women DID work in the idyllic golden age of the American dream, the potential tax stock has almost doubled as a direct result. Jobs which contribute little real wealth creation or productivity—and sometimes hamper productivity—have been created to absorb the new labor supply, such as: HR, bureaucracy, day schools, regulatory & compliance, university administration, etc. That's not to say that much of what is created by the market is *necessary* per se as some goods demanded offer no real utility aside from psychic gain. These goods have been etched into our conscience as essential goods by the Narrative Complex, but do they really ameliorate our lives? Do we really need a new phone with a battery life shorter than a dragonfly's, every 18 months?

In theory, progressive taxation can be a useful method to increase tax revenue equitably. However, it can also be seen as a punative form of taxation, extracting the most resources from the most productive members of society, ridding them of the opportunity to provide more resources to their families in favor of other ends, over which they have no control. In the West, many will celebrate progressive taxation as a net positive but will rarely interrogate the ends to which they are applied. In America, at least, there is a bloated welfare state a thirsty military industrial complex, foreign aid, crumbling infrastructure, numerous superfluous government offices, and several tales of governmental profligacy. Moreover, they can't even balance the damn budget! Not only are they living WELL outside of their means to questionable ends, but they have also run tremendous national debts as well. But, we owe it to ourselves: the children we never had. Do we really think the immigrants imported in lieu of the children we didn't have will take it well when the federal governments debt-based chickens come home to roost?

Another issue with progressive taxation is the incentive structure it promotes. Middle class middle earners may feel less incentivized to put in the extra hours, time away from home, courses, and whatever is necessary to secure a promotion for a few thousand extra bucks a year for more work if they happen to jump into a higher tax bracket. Higher tax rates means less money for the kids. Higher tax rates coupled with devalued currency makes having kids for the average man less affordable. Sometimes, the wife—or husband if the wife is the breadwinner—can't stay at home and give the kids a better upbringing and a tidy, destressed home if finances make it an impossibility. For the more economically disadvantaged, claiming welfare has been almost completely destigmatized in polite society. Having kids has become something of a way of life; except, this time, the breadwinner isn't the father, but the state—the taxpayers who can't afford to have their own kids. What would happen if this wasn't the case, if the incentive structure were to change? We now have a situation where the more enterprising members of society are incentivized to have less children and the more parasitical, morally decrepit, irresponsible, unproductive, and profligate are incentivized to have more children. We can only but conjecture how the future generations will turn out.

Pull Factors

Want something but can't afford it? That's ok, you can just take out a loan or use your credit card. Over the past few decades, in lockstep with the demise of sound money, we have seen a rise in the use of credit cards and short term loans used for a variety of reasons stretching from essential to non-essential ends. The fact is, saving smaller sums has become more challenging due to inflation; therefore, short term borrowing has become more attractive. Having to pay off loans in the future isn't as great a hardship as the material pleasure derived from present gratification. Obviously, in a consumerist society where large corporations also hold great sway over the Narrative Complex, saving money is disparaged by all three heads of the Narrative Complex hydra: Entertainment portrays saving as prudish, consumption as "cool"; Media attacks saving as deleterious to the economy, consumption as fulfilling; Academia scolds saving as hoarding, consumption as something that reflects your authentic being. You're meant to offload your income as soon as it trickles into your account. Be a good consumer. Satisfy your wants with the latest gadget. You have no excuse not to. Furthermore, the need to pay off debts for things such as tuition, medical expenses, car loans, etc, shorten time preferences for many things to a month-by-month basis, rendering future financial planning difficult as funds are extracted for more immediate ends. The easy possibility of debt shortens time preferences and sometimes to catastrophic effect in the example of mushrooming payday loans after the 2008 banking crisis which left tens of thousands in dire straits.

PUSH FACTORS—ECONOMICS
PULL FACTORS—SOCIETY

The State

The modern state—welfare state—is largely responsible for most "push" factors in raising collective time preferences. To continue stimulating the economy, chasing the 3% growth dragon, and tinkering with unemployment by creating superfluous and misguided jobs—arguably a glorified form of welfare—which have been actions heralded as well-intentioned and desirable. By tampering with the economy in order to "push" growth in the short run, collective time preferences rise as money loses its real value. Public spending, which interestingly seems to spike whenever elections are around the corner, promote an illusion of economic activity in the present. Also, around election season, interest rates seem to fall, in some cases, to encourage investment. According to the theory put forward by the Austrian School, as interest rates are a form of price, prices being information, if interest rates are lowered below their natural level (for whatever end), these prices will be distorted and create excess demand for cheap credit—ideally used for long term investment when collective time preferences are low—but, at the same time, in lowering interest rates artificially, more credit in the form of money must enter circulation, raising prices elsewhere, lowering the real value of money and raising collective time preferences.

- Low interest rates should equal low time preferences
- Inflation should equal high time preferences
- Putting two-and-two together equals trouble.

Here, we have a situation where credit (low interest rates), which, ideally should be allocated for longer term projects is now doled out to anyone when current demands, on the whole, require consumption over saving. The misallocation of resources and investment birthed by artificially low interest rates will spell trouble as credit will be issued to unprofitable projects, inevitably causing lay-offs. As a result, we see the phenomenon of bubbles; and bubbles always burst. After economic crises, what the doctor orders may not necessarily be correct. Don't forget, we live in a democracy with an easily duped electorate. Politicians, where elections are held every few years will inevitably be myopic. They're out for re-election. When crisis hits, the panacea is more government spending, lower interest rates, and quantitative easing: all of which would have had a role in blowing the bubble in the first place. This, in essence, only kicks the proverbial can down the road. Eventually, some poor soul will get to this oversized bubble. But, if it weren't for the myopia—high time preferences—of politicians, this could be averted or at least mitigated. When there's mass unemployment, wages stagnating despite rising prices; when breadwinners struggle to provide for their families: they will, naturally, turn to short term solutions—short term solutions for problems which wouldn't exist if it weren't for the self-interest and myopia of bankers and politicians of questionable character. In an abstract pure market economy, those responsible for economic crises would go under and be stripped of their reputation, urging them to act conscientiously; but, of course, we don't live in such a utopia. A banker, who forks out credit irresponsibly to those who cannot realistically repay the bank for temporary gain, isn't punished by a loss of business or status, but bailed out by our governments and handed ample bonuses each successive year in reward. In 2008, part of the crisis was a result of artificially lower interest rates for the sake of delivering affirmative action to groups of people who were, per capita, less capable to complete with the terms of mortgage repayment. What the heck was meant to happen? All of these issues push individuals into having higher time preferences. The incentive structure built up by government policies isn't for civilians to presage far into the future, but to live from moment-to-moment in a form of dependancy making living harder instead of easier.

We often hear about the wonders of "The Nordic System": an advanced welfare state with exorbitant income tax rates. We are frequently told that these countries are among the happiest countries in the world, despite their inordinately high anti-depressant consumption levels. But the tall tales told by the likes of the coastal media are superficial, disingenuous. The wealth created and disbursed by these states was created by private enterprise. There has been no net job creation in Sweden for 55 years. In the early 90s, Sweden's interest rates flew up to 1000% (check) and their debt had to be monetized. Norway, like Saudi Arabia, can afford a generous welfare state due to the wealth generated by fossil fuels. Denmark has among the highest levels of private debt in the world. And, a point often seen on social media, as the mainstream media dare not bring it up: until recently, the small Scandinavian welfare states were relatively ethnically homogeneous, making administration far more sustainable than in a large, polyglot, multireligious, and multicultural nation such as America. Nevertheless, in Scandinavian countries, charitable donations per capita are among the lowest in the western world; removing a sense of humanity or solidarity in the equation as assistance is provided by an impersonal bureaucrat rather than the community.

Throughout one's working life, assuming they work from 25-65, political office will have changed hands several times. In the past 40 years America has had 7 presidents: that is, to say, 7 different administrations; 7 different world views; 7 different sets of morals; several lots of individuals serving their own ends, not wanting to be the fool to inherit any mess. In the case of Ronald Reagan, promising to slash taxes, the size of the federal government increased tremendously. Of course, this comes at a greater cost while recouping less revenue. To continue with the charade, the National Debt must be utilized for smoke and mirrors; who cares, these politicians will be long gone when the debt-based timebomb tocks for the last time. They will never feel the consequences of their actions.

States also contribute towards pull factors in increasing collective time preferences. With subsidies, tax breaks, grants, beneficial regulations, etc, for large corporations who thrive off modern Western consumerism, they are further enabled to produce more abundantly. Some tax rates favor larger corporations over smaller businesses/competitors. The ability to suffer tax burdens in other jurisdictions, thus enlarging net profits allows large corporations to sell their goods at lower prices. Their size allows them to offshore, lobby, and minimize tax burdens abroad, enjoying far greater economies of scale and output. On the one hand, western governments push their citizens into have high time preferences through economic policies designed to look pretty in graphs to elitist economists, and, on the other hand, pull their citizens into higher time preferences by aiding large corporations to produce more consumer goods at a cheaper cost. Westerners are stuck between a rock and a hard place. To appease the Gods of GDP, production—while resources remain finite—must ascend at a parabolic rate to keep up the charade. This is a social death sentence. It is a system which isn't, in the long run, sustainable. As consuming-producers live a sheltered and comfortable life, former suffered hardships now a long-lost distant memory, a massive downturn would prove disastrous as the majority of city-dwellers would be woefully unprepared for such an event.

All of these incentive structures were caused by statesmen with high time preferences themselves. They took kickbacks and power over the wellbeing of their nations because, to them, there would be no consequences: there is no God to judge them in the afterlife, many don't have children who would filter in with the belabored hoi polloi stuck with the consequences of their actions, a corrupt network of self-serving politicians has enabled this practice allowing them to be above the law which they redraft to simply benefit their interests, and a sycophantic Pravda-esque Narrative Complex which covers their backsides shaping their public image so that producing-consumers don't lose trust in these cults of personality. The damage maybe irreversible. Attempting to undo the social and economic policies carefully piled on will be disastrous. No politician will want to inherit another Wall Street Crash. Politicians needing votes in the now, a desperate electorate throughout the West was mislead into taking on Postwar social programs to temporarily alleviate hardship, which now, for many, have sadly become a way of life. Both mainstream wings of the political debate refer to the economy as if it were the lifeblood of a society. This couldn't be further from the truth. It is the people who are the lifeblood of a society—and their economy is a secondary reflection of their culture. Money can't buy a stable harmonious society which gives its people a purpose; but, money can buy politicians.

CHAPTER 14

WHAT CAN BE DONE?

Incentive Structures Sacrifice

FIRSTLY, BEFORE ANY CHANGE CAN BE EFFECTED, we must analyse the incentive structures in our life. Hardship has, for many, become something of the past. Hardship is painful, but must be sought out to remind ourselves than there's more to life than material wealth. Sacrifice and discipline need to be rediscovered. Humility will begin to develop when sacrifice and discipline are practiced; gratification will be sweeter than before if its earned or if one isn't in a constant state of seeking pleasure. With addiction, one goes after greater doses and thrills to satiate their needs; by practicing moderation in gratification, gratification becomes something one can control while being more enjoyable as we're more desensitized or intolerant to such a thing. For example, a pizza is more rewarding as a cheat meal after a month of clean eating and working out than if you were to gorge on them every weekend. But, sacrifice without a purpose is masochism. Sometimes, praciticing sacrifice for the end of tuning one's discipline: for example, I, as a bodybuilder/powerlifter, carry a fair bit of bulk and long distance running can be unpleasant, but I make myself do it on a regular basis to prove to myself that I have control of my body and can willingly do unpleasant things for a greater end, plus, it helps keep undesirable weight gain under control. One of the problems with fitness training—especially if you're natural—is when progress plateaus.

People, if undergoing something challenging, want to see fruits of their labor. Some people simply aren't genetically gifted for lifting, and can train and eat their ass off for months/years to see little gains. They may question if the sacrifice is worthwhile. However, the rewards, even if the gains made are marginal, will certainly outweigh the effort. Consequences to one's actions—short and long term—must become relevant. Nobody likes the pestering know-it-all busybody who nags about consequences to doing X, Y, and Z; but, it should behoove everyone to make sure that undesirable consequences to themselves and others are minimized. With the combination of relatively valueless, hedonistic, and egotistic personal philosophies and the ability to socialize the consequences of one's actions on others; the onus rarely falls on themselves, the individual. By accepting personal responsibility for the consequences of one's action, seeking out sacrifice, giving oneself a purpose, evaluating the incentive structures in one's day-to-day life, and to popularize self-improvement; can we start to lower our time preferences and become less self-centered.

Family

A pervasive sense of hopelessness has come about through a restructuring of incentive structures through the sustained deglamorization of the concept of the nation, faith, and the family. A removal of values greater than the individual has lowered perceived time from beyond one's own lifespan to within one's own lifespan. The societal dissolution of these values—nation, faith, and family—have led modern life into a pit of present-mindedness. Incentive structures based on something less tangible or material will lower time preferences. Intelligence correlates with low time preferences. Intelligence also correlates with lower levels of religiosity. Religiosity and appreciation for less material values do not correlate with with intelligence. Therefore, intelligent people maybe more predisposed to having lower time preferences for material ends, but a greater incentive structure based on something beyond the material maybe necessary to lower time preferences for wider society. Despite the need for incentive structure promoting low time preferences; this incentive structure must be rooted in values that can stand the test of time, transcend social change, and provide a clearly decipherable frame of reference as to how to reinforce best social practices in the future.

The most catastrophic social event to occur to Western Civilization has indubitably been the dissolution of the nuclear family. Marriage has become totally desacralized. Marriage is just another thing on the bucket list; just another step in many loveless, stale relationships. The Narrative Complex hails the end of marriage as one of the many necessary steps to deconstruct the oppressive Western social constructs. As we have every incentive structure making divorce more appealing: you won't face consequences in the afterlife, studies showing the effects on children being raised in broken homes are downplayed by the Narrative Complex, female hyper-gamy has been given an overdose of speed—you go gurl! Don't settle for anything less than a prince!—there's no-fault divorce, women are awarded enormous alimony payments, the children are schooled by others, and marriage is portrayed as dull and stagnant by the entertainment industry. Man the hell up. While it's trendy and exciting to fritter away your youth sowing your oats, it's rarely more satisfying than starting something with substance, love, and a foundation—a foundation to creating a purpose greater than yourself: life. Having children will radically change the incentive structures at hand. One may rethink their universally altruistic politics when they're breadwinners for their family. One may favorite living in a secure, stable environment instead of constantly tracking down new experiences. With risking coming across as a cheesy 80's family movie; there's nothing more important than family. The community, and nation, are extensions of the family. Most individuals scope of being is relatively short and tend not to move far away from where they're born, digging their familial roots deep into the soil. Moving across countries or abroad to pursue a career is a relatively modern phenomenon. Rootlessness, in my opinion, is a large contributing factor towards a sensa-tion of angst experienced by city-dwellers; many of whom proudly state they are cosmopolitans, citizens of the world/Europe, etc, but inadequately veil their lack of identity in a largely materialistic—and childless— existence. An oft-seen trend for city workers when they have children is to move to the suburbs: there's a neighborhood watch, a security force, it's away from the high levels of crime and weirdos, there are other parents to form reciprocal and voluntary relations in childcare, a soccer team, and many more benefits in raising a child in a stable and secure environment.

After having children, as I have mentioned, a secure environment is desirable. In which case, wishing for a political structure that protects its citizens from other groups of potentially hostile individuals becomes a priority so that the parents can be luxuriated with said secure environment. Morover, time preferences will be lowered in order to provide for the children in the future: starting a college fund, buying a house with a better garden, taking them on once-in-a-lifetime trips, saving for their marriage, and other things of a similar nature. A child raised in a stable nuclear family is likely to replicate the same environment for their children. Having a family breeds purpose. Family life also renders certain behaviors such as adultery, promiscuity, alcoholism, drug abuse, hedonism, crime, divorce, and profligacy—all high time preference behaviors— threatening to a stable family environment, thus risking the purpose at hand: raising children to your best ability. Additionally, there is no real substantial gratification for low time preferences when it comes to a secure and stable environment for one's children except for peace of mind. Incentive structures which socially punish divorce, single motherhood, adultery, philandering, familial abandonment, and other acts which jeopardize the upbringing of the succeeding generations must become second nature. However, only in a high-trust society could such incentive structures emerge—which, in many cases, is becoming something of a distant memory.

With the death of the nation, death of God, rise of the welfare state, mass immigration, and ready availability of technology and consumer goods, a loss of a sense of community and general depersonalization can be seen throughout many wealthier western countrys. As the nation dies and transforms into a more multicultural, diluted, multifactional economic zone; social trust diminishes. The purpose here isn't to put forward a theological argument concerning the death of God, but to demonstrate how, with the removal of consequences in removing the beyond—the afterlife—along with a binding moral framework as outlined in certain teachings which have lost their divine authority; there seems to be a loss of a uniting common purpose. In an earlier chapter, I mentioned that aside from oneself, most people would only die for causes greater than oneself such as the family, nation, and faith—all causes greater than oneself.

Now, without such purposes, given the onslaught of critique volleyed at all three—family, nation, and faith—many aspects uniting a community, incentivizing individuals to socially invest in spending time with others, have become extracted from the equation.

Instead of bringing forth a selfless universal man, who loves all as their kin; we now have an indifferent, alienated, introverted man who deems their history contemptible. Religion, in the secular age is viewed negatively, but, with religion, the need for an all-encompassing omniscient state is attenuated by the existence of moral pressures exerted by the wider community rather than at the whim of a few bureaucrats.

Furthermore, the extension of life beyond mortal life far extends time preferences beyond a secular realm. By introducing consequences to owns actions, behaviors that may seem improper to certain communities could be minimized by the threat of divine reprimand. Out of all the things I have said in the book, this will perhaps be the most "triggering" to hear: It is my opinion that the vast majority of people need faith in a divine in their lives. Without faith, all hell breaks loose. One ventures to fill the void with self-destructive means which downward spiral out of control at times. Nothing quite fills the gap. It appears that those who pursue ends to self-effacingly benefit humanity are never quite satisfied. Some cavalierly work on their career in an act of self-deification but squander all their energy on relatively insignificant status and a few extra digits on a screen at the bank in exchange for faith and/or starting a family of their own in a futile self-martyrdom. It's very difficult to put toothpaste back in the tube and Christendom has been in a state of decline for centuries; however, returning to religion may help in finding purpose in life. Of course, secular society looks askance at Christianity above all other faiths due to the rabidly anti-Western Narrative Complex viewing it as a bulwark against the integration of various creeds and cultures wishing to establish themselves in the West. To admit to one's peers that they wish to return to the church may be met with protest. But attempting to add value to one's life by finding things that give them purpose, whatever it may be, will be worth the hassle in the long run. A realization that nothing will quite fill the void, and, in the long run, there needs to be a metaphysical incentive structure to accompany a material incentive structure to add value and given a deeper purpose to one's life—aside from self-aggrandizing individualist philosophies—to stave off soul-crushing emptiness. Low time preferences aren't necessarily a natural condition. Sometimes, there needs to be something greater than oneself to make living beyond today more appealing in the form of a higher, perhaps immaterial, purpose.

A feature which closely follows purpose is responsibility or duty. With responsibility and duty, trust needs to be assigned to the individual in question. Trust confers a sense of belonging; belonging that, along with identity, has been relegated to a thing of the past. An example of responsibility or duty could be military service. Along with the responsibility and duty attached to service comes sacrifice, discipline, and camaraderie from military training. Few members of the younger generations will receive any of these desirable characteristics from everyday life. Contact sports are a fantastic way to build some of the characteristic earned through military service. Rugby, for example, involves discipline, toughness, strength, camaraderie, and responsibility with set roles—and anyone can play. Some forms of hardship don't necessarily have to be painstaking given the fact that there will be a future gratification. In the case of rugby, training hard and eating well may become repetitive or nasty at times, but the future gratification in winning games, excelling at your position, building friendships, or given a purpose—on the rugby pitch, at least—will eclipse the effort spent on honing your skills.

Return to Sound Money

This particular action, in our current world, is impossible; however, I'll suggest it anyway. Returning to hard money; money backed by a commodity or specie (Eg: gold/silver/precious metals), making expansions of the money supply difficult and/or illegal is one way to eliminate many—if not all—push factors in raising time preferences. As I have explained in my chapter on Economics, phenomena such as inflation for low-to-middle income earners places downward pressures on their disposable incomes and discourages savings in favor of short-term expenditure/consumption. Deflation is to be avoided like the plague, but, in pre 1929 economic panics wages would drop but at a far lower rate than consumer prices, indicating that disposable incomes actually increased despite dropping. A return to sound money on a societal scale would involve a major economic crash as all malinvestments would be revealed when interest rates return to the natural level. A crash of such a nature would, inevitably, cause a power vacuum, which, invariably, like all vacuums, need to be filled by something—irrespective of its being better or worse. Moreoever, returning to sound money would see a massive global restructuring of productivity, demand, and could possibly plunge nations whose economies may be reliant on industries such as tourism. However, keeping a check on gradual inflation would see individual value scales be rearranged and to make savings more attractive, promoting low time preferences. If the money in a consumer's pocket retains its value, a greater disinclination to offload their depreciating tender for material goods/experiences, which hold onto their intrinsic value for long than paper money, will become revealed. Certain push factors encouraging consumerism would be eliminated by a return to sound money.

Scaling back welfare—or, as I would hypothetically prefer, in an ideal world, a total abolition—would be political suicide in a modern democracy. In Britain, at least, any talk of cutting benefits is met with a furore of invective and castigation, earning such calumnies as "austerity measures". Dependency is running amok. The incentive structures attached to continuing this glorified political Ponzi scheme have been immeasurably detrimental to the social fabric of Western society—not to mention the adjoining rise in births out of wedlock, contributing towards a lower-trust and alienated society. A mainstream contempt for personal responsibility has followed the cancerous growth of the modern nanny welfare state. Nothing is ever one's fault—unless you're a straight white male, that is. But, what are the incentive structures promoted by a generous welfare state and an inflationary economy designed to maximize a sustainable growth. Like it or not, we've drifted in a technocratic dystopia where individuals are valued by their marginal productivity/utility and ability to consume. In a semi-humanist trance, we've conned ourselves into believing egalitarian fantasies of equal and unlimited potentialities; daring not to question the feasibility of offloading billions of dollars into the hands of the irresponsible, the profligate, and the dependent at the expense of the opposite. In order to raise the downtrodden, the rest of society must also be trodden upon. These aren't desirable ends, short or long term.

Another negative feature of the modern welfare state is that it extirpates a sense of personal altruism and duty as it is "taken care of" in being stealthily extracted directly from your income. The nagging sense of giving and charity as duty is dulled. A more voluntary—and efficient—method of providing assistance to those truly in need, is in order. It would offer a wonderful opportunity for communities which have fallen by the wayside to flourish, to restore their former pride and cohesion. More traditional and communal methods of alleviating extreme hardship to the point where families aren't in a constant survival mode can be implemented to revive their self-respect as well as bring the aid they desperately need. Also, putting a face to those who provide you with sustenance in dark times will discourage freeloading to such an extent. More of a sense of guilt and pressure to get people back on their feet should recreate an incentive structure to not become a long-term burden on one's neighbors or friends. Irresponsibly having many children out of wedlock, which tragically, as become a lifestyle choice for some; will become less attractive once funds to such lifestyles are reduced to only the bare essentials. By removing such political ammunition—which has radically altered western incentive structures to dire effect—a sense of community, solidarity, and independence should reappear in many disaffected, deindustrialized towns. Simply enough, politicians shouldn't be able to buy votes by promising largesse at the expense of others who are vilified as exploiter. Politicians shouldn't be able to win elections by changing the demographics of a nation to suit their empty brand of hollow redistributionism—at the expense of the pre-existing domestic population, that is.

Many politicians—left, right, and "libertarian"—have begun flirting with the idea of universal basic income. At the current time, it seems to be an honorable and necessary government program to cut welfare expenses and to eliminate hampering poverty. Deindustrialized towns ravaged by the fabricated opioid crisis would welcome such a new program. Calls to raise the minimum wage to absurd levels will inevitably cause unemployment and for smaller businesses to suffer in competing with large corporations. Automation is set to claim a number of unskilled/low-skilled jobs and a fallback in the short-term may be necessary to prevent Great-Depression-scale mass unemployment. With UBI and automation, questions about incentive structures and future generations must arise. Firstly, what incentive structures will a guaranteed UBI promote? A great deal of low income earners may find it undesirable to work extra hours for marginally greater pay and significantly reduce their labor hours, thus reducing productivity. An actively unemployed population will grow. When they have children—a lot of whom at the expense of others—will they, on the whole, be raised to adopt an irrepresible work ethic and an insatiable thirst for knowledge, or, alternatively; will a growing underclass of dependents whose growing needs at the expense of a shrinking tax stock outweigh the supply with their demand? Then what? Incentive structures should exist to empower individuals, not to pamper them and to maternally shield them from the consequences of their actions. At the same time, certain families may be marginally better off to the point where a stay-at-home parent may become affordable as a consequence of UBI. Moreover, the introduction of UBI may render certain bureaucratic jobs redundant as part of a restructuring and streamlining process of the welfare state, removing parasitical jobs in the process. There is a lot of anger among the younger generations—and rightly so. They feel swindled for the mess they have received from the preceding generation's high time preferences and postponement of consequences which has left them to shoulder the multitudinous burdens of their forebears. They feel vengeful. And this is a means by which they can exact vengeance, financially. But, in the current, with a social repudiation of discipline, the surgical removal of social consequences to one's actions, and an increasingly unsatisfactory job market for many younger generations; the appeal of UBI will be irresistible—and rightly so, unfortunately.

In the first world, discipline has to be sought out. We have everything at our disposal to avoid discipline like a leper. Finding discipline with tangible rewards to begin a lifestyle where pleasures are earned, not taken for granted, will be a step in the right direction. A purpose is crucial before undertaking a task that requires discipline. Marriage, for example, requires discipline: for better or worse, to make a commitment to a person whose looks, personality, and interests might change over the years in order to raise a family takes discipline and repetition. Falling on hard times, for whatever reason, must be overcome rather than stumbling over hurdles and calling it a day. There are plenty of utilities at one's disposal to keep the marriage together, such as: counselling, self-help guides, courses, etc. Of course, this becomes a greater challenge when both are working, doing chores, and half-heartedly raising children in a state of permanent fatigue. Reevaluating one's values, identifying purposes, and setting doable goals would make deferring gratification and discipline more attractive; however, sacrifices need to be made. Sacrifices are undesirable, especially when people are coaxed into believing that they can have it all and the possibilities are endless—why tie yourself down? Unfortunately, coming to terms with one's humanity and limits is petrifying for many. Most overvalue their capabilities. Identifying what you can and can't do is a necessary step before you can overcome yourself and life's obstacles, rather than quiting when the going gets tough.

This next proposition may sound ridiculous to some,

but moving to the countryside with a set purpose in mind can definitely be of great help to achieve rewarding goals. Sure, there won't be the same amenities, nightlife, bar scene, malls, or whatever other material pleasures are to be offered, but the spiritual gain will be unparalleled. Now, many jobs can be done remotely which removes the need to commute in a cattlecar to a brightly illuminated office for a soulless job; you can now do that soulless job from the comfort of your home. Living in major cities provokes claustrophobia; makes you crave to be elsewhere; crave to be surrounded by life which isn't just dour urbanite commuters, IPA-sippers, or burnt out careerists. Being able to watch seasons transition into each other resembling a life cycle, animals coming and going, plants, feeling crisp air caress your skin; time runs a different pace, a time that is easier to tame, have flow through your fingers, to value. Growing one's own food, or at least having a vegetable garden, will instill discipline and an appreciation for the course of time. Undertaking a repetitive strain of performing tasks on a yearly basis per each seasonal cycle assists in enjoying the direct fruits—or vegetables—of one's labor. Peace and quiet somewhat eliminates stress from achieving one's goals. A more communitarian, regional view of life blooms into belonging and trust over the urban free-for-all sprawl.

Barring a cities amenities, the country provides a superior space to raise a family as children become more attuned to nature and life itself. A purer life-affirming existence can be found in the country despite opposite current trends which liken city life to the highest form of being and intellect. Countryfolk are toothless hicks and don't breathe the same polluted rarified air breathed by the city-dwelling elites. In the country, things move at a slower pace. Despite seasonal changes, values are more stable. Removing a commute or stress caused by city life—which also require destressing in the forms of many escapes in the form of consumerism—can lead one to free oneself from additional problems raised by city life. Country living reforms incentive structures by removing many of the consumerist outlets for dealing with living in a city. Obviously, country living isn't for everyone as the change in living standards could be too overwhelming. However, it offers a means by which to escape the spiritually crushing consumerist carousel of most major cities.

Turn Off Your TV. Now.

They always say that there's nothing good on TV. They're right, there's nothing good on TV. The Narrative Complex, as we know, uses TV to amplify their radical politically-laden narratives in the form of news or entertainment. Either way, life on this worldly plane is *short*, why spend it on something so meaningless, putrifying, vapid, trashy, harebrained, soul-destroying, demoralizing, addictive, brain-addling, unfunny, stultifying, and whatever else. Other things can be done. With the rise of technology, knowledge has been relegated to the technological ether. The average person reads pitifully little—and, why would they? TV is more "fun". Reading is boring. A sort of bizarre egalitarian culture has developed around vilifying self-study as nerdish, to "ya tink ya betta dan me?", to Pol Pot's genocidal tendencies. There is a revulsion of the superior. The high rising poppy must be cut down for the other poppies to continue living in their back-patting fantasy which allows them to enjoy unearned self-pride for another disappearing moment. Again, it's easier to pick up the remote to find something as mentally stimulating as a coma to anaesthetize reality until crawling out of bed to rejoin the rat race. Picking out a book can be an escape, but opening new realms of knowledge is daunting, like facing an unscalable precipice with tumbling boulders streaming down. However, like with all rewards, the reward of opening one's horizons is difficult to value—the value is derived by the continual process of self-overcoming and achievement. That's not, to say, that any book will do. Older books have remained untainted by the conspicuous narrative-bending by the modern Narrative Complex. Older books illustrate a more authentic picture of life and history without trying to construct an existence that isn't quite. Granted, the language maybe more abstruse or harder to decipher, but the reward will be greater. Questioning what you read in the press or finding alternate sources will keep your mental muscles pumped. Challenging your world view and reading literature from opposing views reinforces your beliefs and acts as a repellent to relativism. The NarrativeComplex also blocks a return to older family-centric values or values where the deferral of gratification is brought to the fore. By ferociously denouncing authors, launching ad hominems, and suppressing the dissemination of their work; authors with contradictory vistas to the prevailing narratives are buried as they pose a risk akin to a gust of wind to the intellectual house of cards tirelessly protected by the Narrative Complex—yet they're never afraid to make allusions to Nazi book burning. The Narrative Complex rules out other life-styles which may have added greater value than the modern day bacchanalia which passes as gratifying. Turn off your TV, asphyxiate the Narrative Complex by reducing their air time. Picking holes in their stories isn't hard to do. Their fanatical dogma for their ideals has revealed to many that they have no clothes.

It's difficult to put toothpaste back in a tube. A nut cannot be unbust. There are points of socio-political no return. Modern day conservatism is marked by apathy, appeasement, concessions, and return. By return, I mean returning to core principles that supposedly were, such as laissez-faire economics or a 50's family structure. Conservatism is the art of being on the defensive while defending a poorly guarded redoubt that the bottom of a deep valley—it doesn't stand a chance. Modern main-stream conservatism is nothing more than an annoying stumbling block to progressivism. It isn't proactive, it is barely reactive, it is barely alive as many have become cognizant of its unimpressive legacy. Additionally, it acts as a means to dilute a more unpalatable form of politics which makes it easier to stomach for the average person. Recently, we've seen a rise in the Narrative Complex trying to normalize extreme sexual preferences such as pedophilia and bestiality. The way things are going, we'll probably see dinosaur right-wing outlets champion 'based' pedophiles as stalwarts of free market economics and bastions of conservatism. The mainstream right goes to extraordinary lengths to prove that they're not racist by demonstrating that it is, in actually fact, the left, who is racist. Anybody can become a conservative, but the voting data says otherwise. Trying to take the moral highground in a no-holds-barred political cagefight is a surefire way to lose. Furthermore, since before the Labor Movements, the left has managed to masterfully exploit collective human energy in securing their own political ends.

The left's dialectical genius to rile up support, has been, and will continue to be, an invaluable political tool. The game is checkers, not chess. There will, for as long as people live, always be inequality. The have-nots will always envy the haves, and, for this reason, given the enormous excrescence in material wealth, we've witnessed multitudinous micro civil rights movements crop up out of obscurity to fight for their plight. Our political climate rewards victimhood over accomplishment. There is a clear incentive structure to gain clout and status by playing the oppressed victim. Also, by monopolizing the Narrative Complex to magnify these ideas targeting young adults who've been raised by the Narrative Complex; there's an endless source of political energy to be seized. Permanent revolution, never letting the dust settle is the best way to always secure power and to never become obsolete as politicians. Once welfare has been promised, once gay marriage has been legalized, once growing pot is decriminalized, once infrastructure isn't crumbling, then what? What happens to the career politician? How will they stay relevant? There's always the need for some awful inequality to be rectified. There's always a political crisis which can tug on the bleeding heartstrings of the young—which is why the voting age must be lowered! Conservatives salivating over a Reaganite/Thatcherite political legacy are disconnected from reality. Conservatives are out of touch in this respect and need to gravitate back to planet earth. Although they remain ardent stalwarts of free market capitalism, it doesn't take long to look around and see where big business' ideological sympathies lie— it ain't very conservative. Very few people are passionate about bombing the crap out of the Middle East, especially when troops are mutilated and killed in return for... erm... hmm... not much, really. Promoting family values is outdated, especially when you can have consequence-free sexual intercourse with any consenting partner. Mainstream conservatives are their own worst enemy—but don't even know it.

They haven't a clue to gain support. One line cliches, owning libt*rds online, and muh small government principles isn't enough. Time's have changed. Trump's unprecedented popularity in 2015-2016 was due to the fact that he answered a lot of the white working and middle class' concerns, and he could comandeer a political energy that had been brewing since Bush Sr. When millions have seen their industries offshored, their neighbors resemble a different country, happiness dip, prosperity curtailed, intolerant permissiveness prevail— in the sense than only the most extreme forms of tolerance towards non-traditional lifestyles and sexual preferences must be forcibly accepted, while desanctifying others—it's utterly inevitable that a silent, alienated "basket of deplorables" will be invigorated. Aside from oneself, the only things people would die for are their family, nation, and faith: the nation being an extension of the family and faith is, on the whole, specific to a homogeneous nation or sub groups. It all starts with the family. Everything else is secondary. This is why the family is being destroyed. Energy will come when people become conscious of the fact that their families are being—a priori—ripped apart to fulfill a political agenda. Centering one's political thesis around the family is an interminable source of energy. Putting family first is the only way to reconstruct trust, solidarity, and cohesion. Family life needs to be recaptured and perceived to be desirable. As long as the Narrative Complex has free rein to defecate on family life, from a great height, everyday; people will continue to pursue lifestyles which will ultimately immiserate them.

Without craving family, energy will be squandered on superfluous and trite ends. Attempting to rekindle the passion for an extinct way of life will go the way of the dodo. Making concessions or bending the knee to false notions of social progress merely serves to thoroughly bastardize the initial mission. The church, for example, in many regards has attempted to socially modernize itself to become more appealing to the younger generation. This effort has been wildly unsuccessful despite more traditional branches gaining popularity. After any socio-political movement, its energy will dissipate and gradually extinguish over time. Newer, more energetic, movements will eventually supplant the preceding movements. Conservatism is always fighting a losing battle. Mainstream conservative is a truncated reaction to continual social engineering and consumerism. It doesn't contest the hyper social liberalization since the 1960s, but offers the removal of fetters to the economic policies which enable the possibility of social liberalization. What energy can it muster from the electorate? None. It's mostly a hesitant protest vote. It lives to remain in power long enough in order to make the continued social liberalization palatable enough to continue pushing the social envelope even further, by which time, they are voted out of office. They achieve nothing in regards to lowering social time preferences by assuring a semblance of order or stability. Much of their energy is squandered on trying to get people who viscerally despise them to like them in virtue signaling. Failing this, energy is further squandered by accepting a political moral framework which was constructed to destroy their ability to effect change, then use it against the very individuals who make up the rules. When running candidates, they field inherently unlikeable, out of touch, plutocrats to lead the charge of outmoded politics, thoroughly scorned by everything by everything that resembles what is cool. And they couldn't even defend the family unit—the cornerstone of society. People become more socially conservative when they have children—usually for their children's sake as they crave stability for their children's upbringing, for society not to move at too fast a pace in the meantime.

The energy keeping mainstream conservatism alive are remnants of the 80's neoliberal legacy and a willingness to return to yesteryear. Returning to a racist, bigoted, sexist, yesteryear won't captivate the hearts of the energized young on their quixotic quest to right the world's wrongs—or political right. Facing the choice between a mummified neocon establishment versus a young, hip, lively, affable, relatable, (and browner) Democratic establishment: it's a real tough cookie to the young voter. For there to be energy, there needs to be emotion, NOT REASON, too often. For this energy, the struggle needs to be emotional and relatable. The declawed mainstream conservatism simply cannot relate. How will a character like Jeb Bush stir up the masses into more direct foreign policy, a small tax cut, and tepid platitudes about values? Sounds like an offer too good to refuse. We have to go back to family, fam.

Things done on impulse tend not to have as great a purpose as something long distance. A purpose must be identified before sacrifices be made and pain be endured in order to achieve such end. If incentive structures dampen one's fiery will to delay gratification for a purpose greater than oneself, then the purpose itself becomes devalued. In suffering few to no consequences for one's vices, a person's values and purposes will begin to shift to more immediate and less rewarding ends. Sacrifices are undesirable as they test the limits of one's being while placing restrictions on one's potentiali-ty. A jack-of-all-trades, master of none attitude certainly prevents the realization of one's talents to the fullest. The reality is that rediscovering purposes which provide a certain continuous source of energy to persevere and to have something to get out of bed for. Having low time preferences—which can only come about through foresight, wisdom, strength, perseverance, purpose, pain, sacrifice, and an understanding of consequences of one's actions—assists in bringing order and stability in one's life and in the life of their progeny. The only way to immortalize oneself is by securing a biological legacy—having children. Sure, your essence, your youness, will dissipate over many generations, but it's the only natural means of you living on. Low time preferences for the preservation of your life through your succeeding generations, being a purpose in themselves, making sure they have access to a life of the highest quality. However—however—may it be noted that there lies a temptation to spoil or pamper despite giving them the best headstart which will leave them pitifully unprepared. The upper classes in the final years of civilizations reach a stage of such luxury where hardship is forgotten; they become desensitized to life, sheltered from pain, removed from the world. By living in a state of unnatural comfort, their mental and physical muscles atrophy; they become affected by a heriditary disease which debilitates them beyond repair. They become entitled, have high time preferences, unable to endure hardship, or bother waiting for things. Can you blame them, though? It's very easy to say yes. But their parents raised them ill-equipped for life by providing them with everything they needed, thus ridding them of necessary desires as they had already been taken care of. What is their incentive structure when they can get their hands on anything they want without having to wait around? Over time, life itself—and it's continuation via children—becomes wholly burdensome. Life gets in the way of enjoyment. But life exacts its revenge.

Life doesn't stick around long to those who live it fast. Ironically, it is said that boredom is the absence of pain. In boredom, time goes slowly. In fun, time passes quickly—as a kind of catalyst towards death. But we try to avoid boredom as much as possible. Boredom is stasis, an absence of life or angst, but our perception of life slows down. We feel most alive when we have near brushes with death. When life revolves around fun, it has no substance; likewise, a boring life is one that isn't lived. Overwhelmed by choice, our incentive structures promote fast life, no consequences, live today like there is no tomorrow, no pain, no angst, no necessary sacrifices. It's not really life, it's a fancy method of pressing the fast forward button to welcome death. All good things come to those who wait. Having something greater than yourself, to wait for, may convince you to take your finger off the fast forward button and to just press play.

Finding enduring values as a means to anchor oneself in the sea of propaganda and relativism to give oneself an objective, a direction. In the absense of God, values are lowered to the human, and eventually to the individual, ushering in a form of solipsism. This book isn't an apologetic and I won't try to convince you to believe in a divine, but unearthing enduring values to stand the test of time, to be passed onto your children, and to be greater than yourself as a crutch to live a life worth living amid the rampant hollowness, misery, meaninglessness, alienation, and disaffection which passes as contemporary living.

Dostoevsky pointed out that the most intense lover of humanity detests the individual. The acting individual disrupts the idea of an abstraction of humanity as a whole, as the individual pursues their own end, being out of the control of the the lover of humanity—'humanitarian with a guillotine' is an old phrase for said lover of humanity. Many advocates of ideologies which idolize the abstraction of humanity, as a whole, turn sour pretty quickly as its proponents view themselves as the highest value, forming cults of personality in a process of self-deification. Now these cults of personalities have been both democratized and commoditized, lessening their immediate impact. Don't forget to pick up your T-shirt proudly endorsing your preferred candidate who will lead us to a bright future—lasting 3-8 years until those nefarious scumbags from the other political party gets in power. Politicking isn't really a value in itself. Politics—or the prevailing socially-accepted politics to be more precise—has, as I've previously mentioned, a highest value in itself, elevating self-serving politicians into deities. These aren't heroic individuals to be elevated, but should-be outcasts who would play no significant role in saner, more future-oriented, societies due to the risk they pose from their dangerous levels of extreme narcissism. Finding true lasting values, greater than yourself, which aren't placed on politicians who only serve their interests is a starting place. Your family, your health, your community, your nation, your culture, and their implied survival can become values that outweigh the desire for immediate gratification. When taking the view of the inauthenticity of modern life, rebelling against one's own genetic preservation in favor of meaningless thrills, to only concern ourself with production and consumption, we've never had it so good, but the triumph of the unimaginable material luxury we enjoy is seemingly a Pyhrric victory. Reconnecting oneself to the past will certainly be a vital aid to discovering values worth clinging onto.

The past in itself cannot be changed and it's foundational to getting to terms with who we are. Removing the narrative's lens in viewing the past will reveal to somebody as to why values were non-negotiable. To consider how values were preserved for centuries through bloodshed and suffering that can, ironically, only be recreated by the Narrative Complex to illustrate how unspeakably dreadful it was by today's standards, only for those values to be discarded like yesterday's garbage over a remarkably short period, is quite something to behold. Westerners have lost their self-confidence. Their past is off-limits, their present is despised, their future is forbidden.

Fight through the Negative Incentive Structures

The blueprints to your incentive structures need to be redrawn to reflect a higher, less material living. Sometimes taking the high road is very difficult if you're being pulled down by the prevailing socially-accepted politics and its appetizing incentive structures. Finding meaning or experiences which are outside the orbit of prevailing socially-accepted politics and living a life that doesn't coincide with many of the narratives native to your favorite TV shows. The mainstream narrative and incentive structures need to be transcended. And it won't be without consequence. Consequence is a part of transcendence. Like water off a duck's back, the strange looks shot at non-adherents to the prevailing socially-accepted politics as well as the meaningless insults should fluidly slide off. Stand among others too weak to live beyond the present. There's little that can be done to avoid Push factors for one's incentive structures as they are largely out of the control of the individual. Pull factors, however, can be treated with distrust and abstinence.

One is better than succumbing to the temptation of a cheap thrill over future reward. Pull factors such as entertainment, advertisement, social trends, etc, can avoided when a greater, higher valued, purpose is in mind. Finding a higher value or a reason to keep one on the 'straight and narrow' to mitigate the temptation of Pull Factors is essential to prevent relapsing into the consumerist rut. Moreover, one needs to be able to conceptualize the greater gratification available by forgoing present consumption in favor of future con-sumption. Being able to identify the greater value in a higher value requires intelligence and willingness to change, otherwise, no self-improvement in parrying away temptation to consume will be desirable. If the gratification derived from adhering to a set of higher values cannot be conceptualized to be greater than the will-to-gratification, then no change will be made. Previous values—family, faith, nation—have been thoroughly demonized by the Narrative Complex, not only reducing their value, but inverting them to anti-values; ends to be avoided and fought against. As part of the prevailing socially-accepted politics' values, historically received values now become the enemy of the prevailing socially-accepted politics adherent, thus in mortal combat with their own individual authenticity. Why would the future matter if your adopted values are diametrically opposed to your received identity? The adoption of these values are a form of self-erasure, collective death, per se. The future isn't worth having, therefore, let's cram as many dopamine-soaked experiences until we croak.

Living within one's means where possible—as simple as that sounds—will also limit both the possibility for chaos to seep in and to defer gratification which will increase the enjoyment of gratification in itself. Saving for a car, for example, rather than taking out a loan with steep repayments will lead to a greater sense of reward and accomplishment. Although made increasingly difficult through Push factors—such as inflation or taxation—saving, creating a nest egg, is a means by which financial chaos, stress, and high time preferences can be reduced. Living within one's means seems devastatingly simple to live by, but certain sacrifices such as choosing where one lives, whose one's friends/spouse may be, and the constant temptation of the possibility of securing credit to plaster over stretches of time which the consumer is unwilling to wait; can add to the challenge of living within one's means. Moreover, most people will never be able to afford to buy their first homes outright in the current economy—despite the amazingly high GDP(!)—therefore, taking on mortgages will be unavoidable. However, for most striving towards the completest elimination of personal debt should become a priority to focus their division of their time and efforts towards less material ends.

Finding an antidote to the chaos of modern living will be key in lowering time preferences. As every-thing—both tangible and intangible—is constantly changing at an unprecedented rate, how are values sculpted out of all the noise which constitutes consumer demands? We've moved beyond truth. Truth is now subjective, apparently. We should use our feelings to navigate ourselves through complex scenarios requiring nuance rather than logic, according to the press. And they're not wrong; most people act on feeling rather than fact. If it's all relative—truth, morality, culture, behavior, ability—then what's the point of engaging in activities beyong merely secure safety and survival; as John Lennon would put it: "living for today"? Our wills are many. Most incentive structures in Western Societies today represent a chaotic free-for-all, pandering to every vice, vandalizing virtue. By wading through the deafen-ing noise of relativism and advertisement urging you to loosen your inhibitions in order to consume; arriving at something worth deferring gratification for will provide greater meaning to modern life. Finding stability through constant change will endow you with a greater position to face the day. Chaos is inevitable, but attempting to minimize its effects by avoiding sources of chaos such as TV and toxic individuals should help to make deferral of gratification a more appealing option over immediate gratification. And, don't forget to tidy your room, Bucko!

Debunking the Narrative

Breaking through the narrative's conditioning and reforming one's values is imperative before restructuring incentives. Just by turning off the TV, one will feel a lot better both mentally and psychologically By changing the flow of information in one's life and by filtering out revised histories; one can begin to find reasons to work to a future they might not live to enjoy themselves, but for posterity. The narrative only serves to cast a nihilistic yoke to despair the individual into becoming a formless, fungible consuming-producer. A nihilistic society is one that has no reason to be mad at their social situation since it won't matter what they do to try to change it.

If a consuming-producer dies, he/she can be replaced. Finding a reason to live beyond oneself is part of the process of individuation to leave a long-lasting legacy of the impact left behind by the individual. If one lived a life which practically directly contradicted the narrative, they'd undo much of the toxic pumped out by the Narrative Complex. To realize that what they say is at odds with reality is the first part to cure the constant cognitive dissonance. After that, simply living for today reveals itself as hollow, vapid, pointless. Freeing oneself from the IC bear trap, while daunting, will create a sense of freedom to be. One of the problems is, like X-Files, people want to believe. People want to believe the mainstream narrative because, weirdly, it gives purpose and a sense of belonging. We are social animals, being ostracized is a dreadful feeling. Most people need interaction with others. Being against what the prevailing socially-accepted politics represents can see one being shut out from polite society. Therefore, there are incentives to agreeing with the prevailing socially-accepted political narrative even if, deep down, you think the narratives are baloney.

You're not flawed for your history. You're not inherently evil for your history. Your history is your own and no Ivory Tower establishment pseudointellectual should browbeat you into believing otherwise. What will happen to you if you ignore the past? Will you float in the abyss for all eternity? What a nasty fate! Selectively ignoring the way in which the media represents how you should live is a great place to start. Take on duty and responsibility. Rediscover your self-respect—or simply discover it. There's always room for improvement. You can learn discipline. Meet somebody worthwhile. Start a family. Work your ass off for them. When you're 60, staring down a windy road of physical and mental decline, would you prefer to face it alone or surrounded by people you love and to pass down elements of yourself when your clock runs out? The narrative peddled by the Narrative Complex convinces individuals to despise themselves through constantly bashing one's history and heroes, and then to heal from their artificially inflated self-hatred through meaning-less, destructive debaucherous consumerism. It is by design. The Narrative Complex' sophists will have their bare bottoms revealed as soon as their wishy washy intellectual con is exposed. Mining excuses for one's poor life choices through abstruse language simply shirks responsibility. Without taking responsibility, one admits that they aren't in control of their faculties or impulses—they renounce their own humanity to avoid dealing with the pain of existence; a pain that can be cured by pulling out the ideological dagger thrusted deep into the backs of the Western conscience by the Narrative Complex. The will to multiculturalize one's nations is an admittance to a loss in self-belief in one's own culture or values, desiring it to become enriched or complemented by others which aren't their's. A sus-tained campaign launched by the Narrative Complex to thoroughly demoralize individuals into wandering blindly into one's own cultural displacement. Food is often clownishly cited as a main reason as to why the west's displacement is desirable. If the odd bespoke foodgasm outranks your valuing of the importance of your nation and the millions who sacrificed their lives for your pampered sorry derriere, life must be so devoid of meaning that crawling out of bed in the morning must be a struggle. Indifference is worse than hatred.

Hatred at least recognizes the existence of a group and an existential conflict. Indifference almost passively, cowardly, wills for its erasure—as the indifferent individual wishes that group to be gone, without a fight, through their own self-disgust but, since they cannot assume responsibility, their will for its erasure is manifested in indifference, rather than active approaches. At the end of the day, it all stems from emptiness. Their poor souls have been crushed by sustained propaganda. And their lives will reflect the malicious narratives propped up by the Narrative Complex: absolutely inauthetic and tormented.

Ignoring the narrative cast by the Narrative Complex by becoming impervious to the state of guilt they try to impose will partially free oneself from presentminded to add value and meaning to the future. Thanks to the toxic sludge that passes as the narrative, we've witnessed several instances of many individuals wishing away their country due to a lopsided anti-Western framework when history is taught. Your people are responsible for the most unspeakable horrors committed and their triumphs aren't of their own as they were stolen from other groups. This narrative is relentlessly pushed on millions. Why would you want to keep the gene pool responsible for the world's most ghastly atrocities alive? You'd better forgo having children, right? Wouldn't wanna carry on pissing in the gene pool to spoil the other swimmers.

Deconditioning oneself from the narrative is quite difficult, especially as the narrative serves to evoke feelings rather than to promote free critical thinking. You can think critically, but within the narrow confines of the prevailing socially-accepted politics. Places which promote these narratives should be avoided unless necessary. Universities are best avoided unless one wishes to pursue a career in stem. The more time that can be spent away from their venomous fangs, the better. There is mutually-sustaining, self-propagating, force between the Narrative Complex and Corporates plus the prevailing socially-accepted political State. Living outside of the false reality—the narrative—to immunize oneself from the consumerist condemnation—high time preferences—is another means by which one can give meaning to their lives and use of physical time.

Nobody, except Westerners, are conned into feeling guilt for their ancestors. Why should you feel guilty? People getting their dopamine rocks off by pandering to minorities and willingly adopting a perverse slave morality, in showing the world how good a person they are, by wilfully sacrificing their countries to the alter of progress—whose destination is unknown. It's a very bold investment to make, facilitated by one's own voluntarily disconnection to their past through consistent propaganda. Guilt should be restricted to one's own actions and the consequences directly by others. Removing guilt like a malignant tumor will lower one's time preferences as there would be less reason to loathe one's own existence and more reason to live beyond the immediate. Guilt implies a recognition for responsibility, and those unwilling to assume responsibility for their actions pose a threat to the integrity of certain groups. Thinking and living solely for today should be made less trendy. That's not, to say, to completely eliminate fun or to avoid gratification altogether. Moderation should be practiced. Passing judgement is a form of care, not an excuse to wield authority. Judging people for where they drift astray should be a self-imposed duty to those who view themselves and their society as a going concern, to reinforce the most adequate behaviors for that social group. Forming groups of likeminded individuals who won't exclusively live for today and who reject the guilt-infested toxic Narrative Complex narrative can also be helpful to adding value/purpose to one's life. Along with discrediting or ignoring the mainstream Narrative Complex narratives would a restructuring of social incentive structures to become more future oriented would be required to fill the void left by the absence of the Narrative Complex narratives. For over three generations has society's narrative been dominated by anti-Western propaganda—practically a living memory. After the fall of the Soviet Union, despite a living-memory's worth of antitheism, Russians returned to the Orthodox Church in droves. After the fall of the Narrative Complex' narrative there will be a demand for another narrative, one more aligned with reality, to take place. The message of deferring gratification without an authentic concern for the future won't be entirely well-received—like a child being told to clean their room. Returning to duty after lengthy dereliction can seem unpleasant. However, Western incentive structures must return to a position where decivilizing high time preferences are negatively viewed to condition optimal behaviors.

A need for a recognition of responsibility to others is the recognition of one's belonging in the world. By shirking responsibility, one is tacitly removing oneself from the picture as there is no implied care or understanding of consequences for one's actions. The same applies with sacrifice: having low time preferences requires sacrifice as other possibilities and potentialities must be excluded or forgone in order to defer gratification. And by deferring gratification arises a greater, monetarily unquantifiable, appreciation for accomplishment. In channeling an adequate amount of discipline to free oneself from their will-to-gratification and impulses, value is added to one's daily activities and to their lives. But it means suffering a little more in the immediate for a greater future comfort—a task which many, sadly, simply aren't up to.

For civilization to last beyond the present, socially low time preferences based on family and the preservation on those self-propagating values is an imperative. If civilization becomes morally and demographically rearranged, it may remain the same civilization geographically, but not the same one culturally. Living for today—and only for today—on a societal scale will sadly spell trouble as there will be little concern for the future. A process of decivilization and cultural decline will be inevitable if the founding values are excised and replaced by an undifferentiated amorphous mass of consumerism and hyper-tolerance. Meaning is difficult to find in the modern world. Brands offer temporary surrogacy for meaning and identity. For reasons to have low time preferences to reveal themselves amid the chaos, narratives, metanarratives, incentive structures, consumerism, vapidity, alienation, and hollowness of living for today, one needs to reconnect with their past as a starting point. We are not meant to be fungible economic units whose raison d'etre is to increase marginal productivity for megacorporations. Time matters: when life has a deeper meaning other than immediate gratification, time horizons lengthen and time preferences lower. Currently, life, for many, is absent of more meaning that the entertainment shows or brands one consumes. Life has got to be worthwhile, to some degree, in order for one to step outside their comfort zone and to live according to something which ascribes life a greater meaning, to the point which they could defer gratification for reasons beyond oneself. Things have to matter more than simple immediate gratification enabled by current incentive structures according to social acceptability, technology, social programs, and wealth. There is more than the present, but, in order for it to matter, a belief in the future and a reason—often greater than oneself—are needed before one can free themselves from their passions.

BIBLIOGRAPHY

Sources:

(1) Obesity –
https://www.gov.uk/government/publications/he
alth-matters-obesity-and-the-food-environment/
health-matters-obesity-and-the-food-environment--2

(2) Bell Curve

(3) Average Salary –
https://www.thebalancecareers.com/average-
salary-information-for-us-workers-2060808

(4) https://www.dailymail.co.uk/news/article-
2270399/Couples-stick-gender-roles-home-sex-20-
times-year.html

(5) Abortions –
https://www.breitbart.com/politics/2019/04/30/n
ew-york-city-babies-aborted-after-21-weeks-
outnumbered-homicides/

(6) https://twitter.com/spectatorindex/status/9412928
29384437761

(7) Brexit Vote – https://www.bbc.com/news/uk-
politics-45098550

ABOUT THE AUTHOR

ORWELL & GOODE (a pun for "all well and good") is a Youtuber, blogger, and an economics masters degree student. His main interests lie in documenting the decline of the Western world and identifying economic policies which may shape society for better or worse. He is the host of the "All Well and Good Show" and the co-host of news round-up "Waking Up The West" on YouTube.

Twitter: @OrwellNGoode
YouTube: Orwell Goode
Facebook: OrwellNGoode

Printed in Great Britain
by Amazon